W9-AUK-030

FLAGSTAFF HIKES

SIXTH EDITION

By

Richard K. Mangum
and Sherry G. Mangum

Look for Our Other Publications

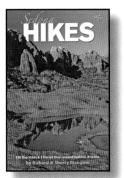

Sedona Hikes

Flagstaff Historic Walk

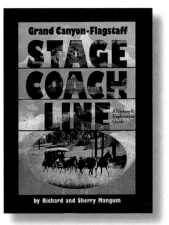

Grand Canyon-Flagstaff Stagecoach Line

NONLIABILITY STATEMENT

While we have worked hard to guarantee accuracy and have personally taken every one of these hikes, errors in field notes, transcription and typesetting can occur. Changes also occur on the land and some descriptions that were accurate when written may become inaccurate by the time you use this book. One storm or forest fire, for example, can change a trail or road. In addition to the problem of accuracy, there is the problem of injury. It is always possible that hikers may sustain harm while on a hike. The authors, publishers and all those associated with this book directly or indirectly, disclaim any liability for accidents, injuries, damages or losses that may occur to anyone using this book. The responsibility for good health and safety while hiking is that of the user.

Cover Design by Joan Carstensen Design, Flagstaff
Cover photo by Sherry G. Mangum:
Summer Wildflowers Near Kendrick Peak

© Richard K. & Sherry G. Mangum, licensed to Hexagon Press, Inc.
All other rights reserved
ISBN 978-1-891517-04-4
6th Edition 2007

Printed in China

Table of Contents

Changes for this Edition

Welcome to the 6th version of Flagstaff Hikes. We are especially proud of this edition because it realizes a dream we have had since 1992 when we published our first version: to produce the book in color. There are several changes that users will notice. The first is that we have a photograph of each hike on the pages describing it. The photo is in glorious color. Second, the map that appears for each hike is in color. The title for each hike is color-coded: red for hard, yellow for moderate, and green for easy, making it simple for users to find the kind of hike they want by flipping through the book.

Another major change is that we have included **GPS waypoints** for each hike. Many of us hike with a GPS these days and having the essential reference points can help in planning a hike or navigating while out on the trail.

The final change is that we have altered the way we present time and distance information. In the five previous editions we have shown the distance one-way only, unless the hike was a loop. Now we show the distance one-way and round-trip with the time both ways, together with the total driving and hiking time. This improvement makes it easier to plan a hike.

We have changed our approach to the selection of hikes. In the past our aim was to include all the worthwhile hikes that a hiker might want to make while using Flagstaff as a base. With this edition we have trimmed the hikes so that they are limited to those within a 50-mile radius of town—with the exception of a few unusual hikes that are worth a longer drive. We are also reducing the number of hikes that call for bushwhacking, so that all of the hikes take place on real trails.

Hikes Deleted from This Edition:

Beyond the 50-Mile Limit: Bright Angel, Calloway, Fossil Springs, General Spring, Horse Crossing, Houston Brothers, Kinder Crossing, Lonesome Pocket, Mack's Crossing, Maxwell, Pivot Rock, Point, Secret Pocket, Tramway, Wildcat Spring, and Willow Crossing.

Deleted for Other Reasons: Antelope Hills, Arizona Trail—Allen Lake, Babe's Hole, Beale Road on Government Prairie, Bear Canyon—Overland Road, Chalender Cross-Country Trails, Coal Mine Canyon, Coconino Rim Trail, Connector Trail, Crater Lake, Elden Skyline Trail, Flagstaff-North Trail, Flagstaff Spring, Government Knoll, Geronimo Spring, Grandview Trail, Hermit Trail, Hutch Mountain, James Canyon, Johnson Crater-Johnson Canyon, Kelsey Spring, Oak Creek Vista, O'Leary Peak, Overland Road, SP Crater, South Kaibab Trail, Sycamore Basin Trail, Three Sisters, Turkey Hills, Walnut Canyon Link, Weatherford Canyon, West Fork Head, White Horse Hills, Wild Bill Hill, Wildcat Hill, and Wing Mountain.

New Trails for this Edition: Arizona Trail—Mormon Lake Railroad, Campbell Mesa Trails, Fay Canyon, Fort Valley Trail, Oldham Trail-Easy, Priest Draw Trail, Schultz Loop Trail, and Skunk Canyon.

Renamed or Realigned: Abineau Canyon, Little Elden Trail, Old Lowell Observatory Road, Oldham Trails, Strawberry Crater Trail, Vista Loop Trail, Wildlife Trail, and Tunnel Road Trail.

About the Authors

Dick was born in Flagstaff. From his childhood he has enjoyed getting out into the woods, canyons, hills and mountains surrounding his birthplace. After graduating from Flagstaff High School, he attended the University of Arizona, where he obtained a law degree. He returned to Flagstaff and engaged in the general practice of law for fifteen years, then became a Superior Court Judge in Flagstaff in 1976.

He retired in November 1993 in order to devote full time to his two favorite hobbies, hiking and writing. He wrote the articles in the book, drew the maps and did the layout.

Dick and Sherry on the Sandys Canyon Trail, November 2006, by Lev Ropes

Sherry has lived in Flagstaff since she was seven years old. Like Dick she enjoyed getting into the outdoors from the time she was a toddler. Inheriting her love for photography from her parents, both professionals, she has refined her skills to produce the photographs used in this book.

Adept at all aspects of photography, she prefers landscapes. Her work has been published in books and periodicals since 1978. She used a 35mm film camera for years but has switched to digital. All her photos in this book are digital. Along with learning to use the camera she has become expert with photo software.

The Mangums have produced ten titles and were awarded the Copper Quill Award by the Friends of the Public Library in 2000 for their significant contribution to the literature of the Flagstaff area. They were also named Flagstaff Ambassadors by the Citizen of the Year Committee of the *Arizona Daily Sun.*

Tips on Flagstaff Hiking

Water

Don't count on finding water any-where. Take all necessary water with you.

High Elevation

Hikes around Flagstaff start at 7,000 feet and go all the way up to 12,633 feet, the highest point in Arizona, at the top of Mt. Humphreys. High elevations mean the following things: 1. You won't have the energy you have at lower altitudes, 2. Hiking will be a lot harder on your heart, 3. You will be drier than usual, 4. You will sunburn more easily, 5. It will be much colder than normal, especially at night, 6. Alcohol is more in-toxicating.

The Terrain

Flagstaff country is generally benign. You can get lost in the woods but you won't if you stay on the hikes described in this book.

Rock Climbing

We do not provide any rock climbing information. There are good climbing sites in the area, however. Check at local sporting goods stores for information.

Varmints

Because Flagstaff is cool and has long winters there are few mosquitoes. Pests like chiggers are absent. Ticks are rare in the high country. There are a few black widow spiders around, but no scorpions. Rattlesnakes live in the area but are not plentiful. Even so, don't do anything stupid like reaching blindly under a rock or into a brush pile.

Weather

Flagstaff's normal snow season is anytime between Halloween and Easter. Don't count on hiking in the high country then. Summers are perfection though rain is common between the Fourth of July and Labor Day. We indicate the best times for hiking with a Weather Report graphic on each map.

Access

Some of these hikes are totally unavailable in winter. Hikes in the high mountains are impossible then because of snow. The average snowfall in Flagstaff is 108 inches and the mountains get even more. Many roads are blocked by snow and the Forest Service closes some of the roads with locked gates during the winter.

Handy Charts & Data

Hours of Daylight

	JAN	FEB	MAR	APR	MAY	JUN	JUL	AG	SEP	OCT	NOV	DEC
SUNRISE	7:35	7:26	6:57	6:14	5:36	5:14	5:16	5:35	5:59	6:21	6:48	7:16
SUNSET	5:26	5:55	6:22	6:48	7:12	7:35	7:45	7:30	6:54	6:11	5:33	5:15

Normal Precipitation in Inches

JAN	FEB	MAR	APR	MAY	JUN	JUL	AUG	SEP	OCT	NOV	DEC
2.04	2.09	2.55	1.48	0.72	0.40	2.78	2.75	2.03	1.61	1.95	2.40

Normal Temperatures—High and Low

JAN	FEB	MAR	APR	MAY	JUN	JUL	AUG	SEP	OCT	NOV	DEC
42.2	45.3	49.2	57.8	67.4	78.2	79.0	79.3	73.2	63.4	61.0	51.1
15.2	17.7	21.3	26.7	33.3	41.4	50.5	48.9	41.2	31.0	22.4	15.8

Conversion Table—Meters to Feet

Meters	910	1212	1515	1818	2121	2424	2727	3030	3333	3636
Feet	3000	4000	5000	6000	7000	8000	9000	10000	11000	12000

How to Use This Book

Alphabetical arrangement. The hikes in this book are arranged from A-Z.

Index. The index starts at page 190. It groups the hikes by geographical area and by special features.

Layout. The text, photo and map for each hike are on facing pages so that you can take in everything at a glance.

Maps. The maps are not to scale but their proportions are generally correct. The main purpose of the maps is to get you to the trailhead. The maps show mileage point-to-point. The text gives cumulative mileage.

Larger scale maps. For the big picture we recommend using a Forest Service recreation map or the Flagstaff Trails Map.

Bold type. When you see a trail name in bold type is means that the hike is described in this book.

Ratings. We show hikes rated as easy, moderate and hard. We are middle-aged hikers in average condition—not highly conditioned athletes who never tire. Hikers should adjust our rating for their own fitness level.

Mileage. Driving distance for each hike is measured from Flagstaff City Hall, located at the junction of Route 66 and Humphreys Street. All hikes start from this point. Milepost locations are also shown on the maps (as MP) on highways that have them.

Access roads. To reach many of these hikes you will have to travel unpaved roads, some of them rough. Our vehicle has 4-wheel drive and good clearance. We based our access rating on how well our vehicle handled the roads.

Safety. We avoid taking risks on hikes. None of these hikes required technical climbing.

Wilderness areas. The Flagstaff area is blessed by having many of its hiking places included within federally designated Wilderness Area. This is great for hikers, as no motorized vehicles or even bikes are allowed inside them.

Cairns. These are stacks of rocks used as trail markers. Some are officially placed, while others are made by hikers. Do not disturb them. Their guidance is needed.

Mileposts. Major Arizona highways are marked every mile by a sign about three feet high mounted on posts at the side of the road. They contain white lettering on a green background.

Our Personal Favorite Hikes
Are Marked With This
Red Ribbon Symbol

Leave No Trace Outdoor Ethics

Plan Ahead And Prepare
• Know the regulations and special concerns for the area you'll visit.
• Prepare for extreme weather, hazards, and emergencies.
• Schedule your trip to avoid times of high use.
• Visit in small groups. Split larger parties into groups of 4-6.
• Repackage food to minimize waste.
• Use a map and compass; eliminate the use of rock cairns, flagging, marking paint.

Travel And Camp On Durable Surfaces
• Durable surfaces: established trails & campsites, rock, gravel, dry grasses, snow.
• Protect riparian areas by camping at least 200 feet from lakes, streams.
• Good campsites are found, not made. Altering a site is not necessary.
In popular areas:
• Concentrate use on existing trails and campsites.
• Walk single file in the middle of the trail, even when wet or muddy.
• Keep campsites small. Focus activity in areas where vegetation is absent.
In pristine areas:
• Disperse use to prevent the creation of campsites and trails.
• Avoid places where impacts are just beginning.

Dispose Of Waste Properly
• Pack it in, pack it out. Inspect your campsite and rest areas for trash or spilled foods. Pack out all trash, leftover food, and litter.
• Deposit solid human waste in catholes dug 6 to 8 inches deep at least 200 feet from water, camp, and trails. Cover and disguise the cathole when finished.
• Pack out toilet paper and hygiene products.
• To wash yourself or your dishes, carry water 200 feet away from streams or lakes and use small amounts of biodegradable soap. Scatter strained dishwater.

Leave What You Find
• Preserve the past examine, but do not touch, cultural or historic structures and artifacts.
• Leave rocks, plants and other natural objects as you find them.
• Avoid introducing or transporting non-native species.
• Do not build structures, furniture, or dig trenches.

Minimize Campfire Impacts
• Campfires can cause lasting impacts to the backcountry. Use a lightweight stove for cooking and enjoy a candle lantern for light.
• Where fires are permitted, use established fire rings, fire pans, or mound fires.
• Keep fires small. Only use sticks from the ground that can be broken by hand.
• Burn all wood and coals to ash, put out campfires fully, then scatter cool ashes.

Respect Wildlife
• Observe wildlife from a distance. Do not follow or approach them.
• Never feed animals. Feeding wildlife damages their health, alters natural behaviors, and exposes them to predators and other dangers.
• Protect wildlife and your food by storing rations and trash securely.
• Control pets at all times, or leave them at home.
• Avoid wildlife during sensitive times: mating, nesting, raising young, or winter.

Be Considerate Of Other Visitors
• Respect other visitors and protect the quality of their experience.
• Be courteous. Yield to other users on the trail.
• Step to the downhill side of the trail when encountering pack stock.
• Take breaks and camp away from trails and other visitors.
• Let nature's sounds prevail. Avoid loud voices and noises.

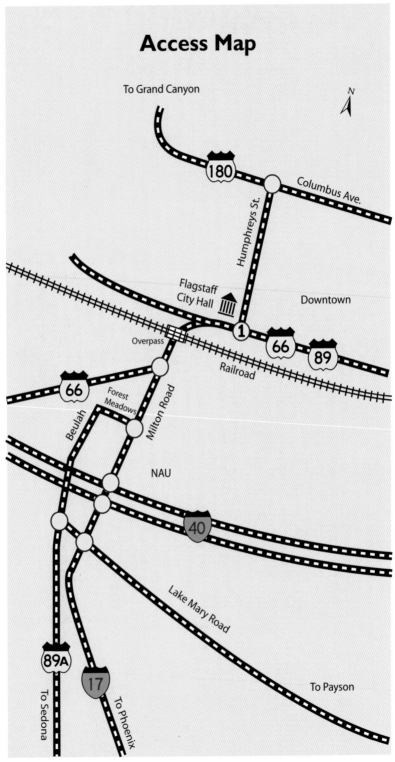

Access Map

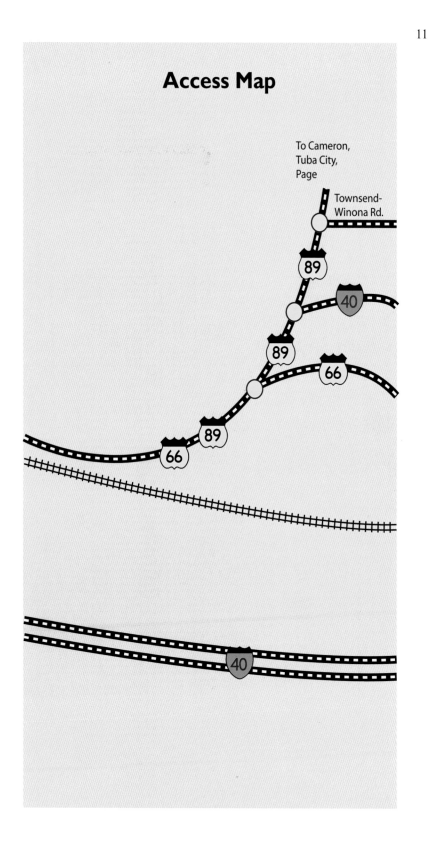

Hike Locator

The references are to the map on the opposite page

B2
Red Mountain

B3
Slate Mountain

B5
Grand Falls

C2
Bull Basin
Kendrick Mountain
Lava River
Pumpkin
Watchable Wildlife

C3
Abineau Canyon
Bear Jaw Canyon
Bismarck Lake
Humphreys
Inner Basin
Kachina Trail
Little Spring
Lookout
Saddle Mountain
Schultz Creek
Schultz Loop
Veit Springs
Walker Lake
Waterline Road
Weatherford Trail
Wilson Meadow

C4
Doney Trail
Lava Flow
Wupatki Ruin Trail

C5
Strawberry

D1
Beale Road
Benham Trail
Bill Williams Mt
Bixler Saddle
Buckskinner
Clover Spring
Davenport Hill
Keyhole Sink
Route 66
Summit Mountain

D2
A-1 Mountain

D3
Brookbank
Buffalo Park
Campbell Mesa
Christmas Tree
Fort Valley
McMillan Mesa
Museum Nature
Observatory Mesa
Rio de Flag
Sinclair Wash
Soldiers Trail

D4
Deer Hill
Elden Lookout
Elden Pueblo
Elden Spring
Fat Man's Loop
Heart
Little Bear
Little Elden
Old Caves Crater
Oldham Trail #1
Oldham Trail, Easy
Oldham, Upper

Pipeline
Rocky Ridge
Sandy Seep
Sunset

E1
Sycamore Rim

E3
Griffiths Spring

E4
Anderson Mesa
Fay Canyon
Priest Draw
Sandy's Canyon
Skunk Canyon
Vista Trail
Walnut Canyon
Wood Trail

F2
Casner Mountain
Dorsey Spring
Kelsey Spring-
Winter Cabin
Secret Mountain
Taylor Cabin
Winter Cabin

F3
Crystal Point

F5
Arizona Trail
–Mormon Lake RR
Lakeview
Mormon Mountain
Railroad Tunnel

Location Map

A1	A2	A3	A4	A5
B1	B2 Red Mountain	B3	B4	B5 Grand Falls
C1	C2 Kendrick Peak	C3 San Francisco Peaks	C4 Sunset Crater Wupatki	C5
D1 Williams	D2 Bellemont	D3 Flagstaff 🏛	D4 Mt. Elden	D5 Winona
E1	E2 Woody Mountain	E3 Griffith Spring	E4 Lake Mary	E5
F1	F2 Mogollon Rim	F3 Munds Park	F4	F5 Mormon Lake

Hikes Grouped by Difficulty

EASY
Anderson Mesa
Arizona Trail
–Mormon Lake
Logging RR
Beale Road at Laws
Spring
Buffalo Park
Campbell Mesa
Crystal Point
Elden Pueblo
Griffiths Spring
Keyhole Sink
Lava Flow
McMillan Mesa
Museum Nature Tr.
Priest Draw
Rio de Flag
Route 66
Sandy Seep
Sinclair Wash
Veit Springs
Walker Lake
Watchable Wildlife
Trail
Wilson Meadow
Trail
Wood Trail
Wupatki Ruin Trail

MODERATE
Bismarck Lake
Buckskinner
Christmas Tree
Clover Spring
Davenport Hill
Doney Trail
Elden Spring
Fat Man's Loop
Fay Canyon
Fort Valley
Grand Falls
Lakeview
Lava River
Little Elden
Little Spring
Lookout Trail
Observatory Mesa
Old Caves Crater
Oldham Trail #1
Oldham Trail Easy
Pipeline Trail
Priest Draw
Railroad Tunnel
Red Mountain
Rocky Ridge
Saddle Mountain
Sandys Canyon
Schultz Creek
Schultz Loop
Secret Mountain
Skunk Canyon
Slate Mountain
Soldiers Trail
Summit Mountain
Vista Trail
Walnut Canyon
Waterline Road
Winter Cabin

HARD
A-1 Mountain
Abineau Canyon
Bear Jaw Canyon
Benham Trail
Bill Williams Mt
Bixler Saddle
Brookbank
Bull Basin
Casner Mountain
Deer Hill
Dorsey Spring
Elden Lookout
Heart
Humphreys
Inner Basin
Kachina Trail
Kelsey Spring-
Winter Cabin
Kendrick Mountain
Little Bear
Mormon Mountain
Oldham Trail Upper
Pumpkin
Strawberry
Sunset
Sycamore Rim
Taylor Cabin
Weatherford Trail

Hikes by Total Drive & Hike Time

UP TO 1 HOUR
Buffalo Park
Elden Pueblo
Museum Nature Tr.

1-2 HOURS
Anderson Mesa
Elden Spring
Griffiths Spring
Lava Flow
McMillan Mesa
Observatory Mesa
Old Caves Crater
Rio de Flag
Route 66
Sandys Canyon
Veit Springs
Vista
Watchable Wildlife
Wood

2-3 HOURS
A-1 Mountain
Arizona Trail
Beale Road, Laws
Bismarck Lake
Campbell Mesa
Christmas Tree
Clover Spring
Crystal Point
Doney
Fat Man's Loop
Fay Canyon
Keyhole Sink
Lakeview
Lava River
Oldham Easy
Priest Draw
Red Mountain
Rio de Flag
Sandy Seep
Schultz Loop
Sinclair Wash

Skunk Canyon
Strawberry
Walker Lake
Walnut Canyon
Waterline
Wilson Meadow
Wupatki

3-4 HOURS
Buckskinner
Fort Valley
Grand Falls
Little Spring
Lookout
Oldham #1
Oldham, Upper
Rocky Ridge
Slate Mountain
Soldiers
Summit Mountain
Winter Cabin

4-5 HOURS
Bixler Saddle
Brookbank
Davenport Hill
Dorsey Spring
Elden Lookout
Mormon Mountain
Pipeline
Saddle Mountain
Schultz Creek
Secret Mountain

5-6 HOURS
Abineau
Heart
Inner Basin
Kachina
Little Bear
Little Elden
Sunset

6-7 HOURS
Bear Jaw Canyon
Bull Basin
Casner Mountain
Deer Hill
Kendrick Mountain
Railroad Tunnel

7-8 HOURS
Benham
Bill Williams
Humphreys
Pumpkin
Sycamore Rim
Taylor Cabin

9-10 HOURS
Kelsey-Winter

10-11 HOURS
Weatherford Trail

A-1 Mountain

Location Map D2
Flagstaff West USGS Map
Coconino Forest Service Map

Driving One-Way/Total: 9.4/18.8 mi. *15.0/30.1 km* (Time 30/60 minutes)
Access Road: All cars, Last 3.9 miles *6.2 km* good gravel road
Hiking One-Way/Total: 1.0/2.0 mi. *1.6/3.2 km* (Time 40/80 minutes)
How Strenuous: Hard   *Total Drive & Hike Time:* 2 hrs. 20 min.
Features: Landmark mountain north of Flagstaff

NUTSHELL: A steep climb up the east face of A-1 Mtn., where you enter its crater through the blown-out east side, then climb to the rim.

DIRECTIONS:
From Flagstaff City Hall (1) Go:
    West a block on Route 66, then south, beneath the railroad overpass, see Access Map, page 10. At 0.5 miles *0.8 km*, a Y intersection, turn right on Route 66. At 5.0 miles *8.0 km* you merge onto I-40 West (2). At 5.3 miles *8.5 km* take Exit 190 (3). Turn right at the stop sign (4) onto road FR 506. Follow 506 to the 7.5 mile *12 km* point, where you will meet FR 515 forking to the right (5). Go left here on FR 506, the main road. At 7.9 miles *12.6 km* go left at a fork on FR 518B (6). At 9.4 miles *15.0 km* you arrive at the trail, a closed jeep road, to your left, 35°13.807'N 111°43.629'W. The road is designated FR 9218-D. Park nearby, where the old radio facility (razed) was located.

TRAILHEAD: No signs. Just walk the jeep road uphill.

DESCRIPTION: A-1 Mountain is a basaltic volcano with a nicely shaped crater, breached where part of its east side blew out. There was an extensive lava flow from A-1 Mtn., seeming almost disproportionate to its smallish size. The lava flow advanced about 4.0 miles *6.4 km* to the east where its abrupt edge forms the 200-foot tall hill behind the Museum of N. Arizona and all along the west side of town. Lowell Observatory sits atop the lava flow near this edge.
    The path climbs moderately at first, then you make a steep scramble (poor footing here) to descend into the crater. In the crater at 35°14.135'N 111°44.011'W you can hike a gravel road to the right going up to the northeast rim. Or you can follow the trail around the basin and up to a higher point on the west rim at 35°14.065'N 111°44.200'W. Both points have restricted views due to tree cover.
    The Arizona Cattle Company ranched in this area from 1885 to 1902. Its brand was the A-1, which is how this mountain got its name.

Photo: Although this is generally a steep trail, parts of it are level and provide a lovely walk through inviting woods.

A-1 Mountain

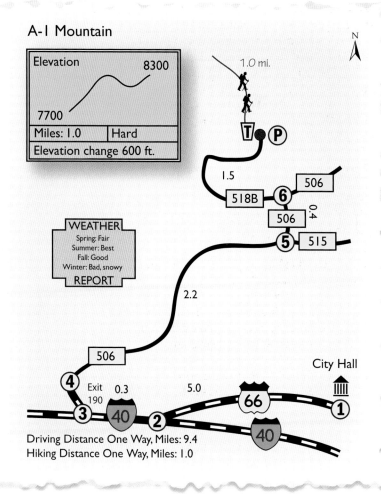

Elevation

8300

7700

Miles: 1.0	Hard
Elevation change 600 ft.	

1.0 mi.

T ● P

N

1.5

518B — **6** — 506

506

0.4

5 — 515

WEATHER
Spring: Fair
Summer: Best
Fall: Good
Winter: Bad, snowy
REPORT

2.2

506

City Hall

4

Exit 190   0.3

5.0

3 — **40** — **2**

66

40

1

Driving Distance One Way, Miles: 9.4
Hiking Distance One Way, Miles: 1.0

Abineau Canyon #127

Location Map C3
Humphreys Peak and White Horse Hills USGS Maps
Flagstaff Trails Map©

Driving One-Way/Total: 24.3/48.6 mi. *38.9/77.8 km* (Time 50/100 min.)
Access Road: All cars, Last 5.3 miles *8.5 km* fair gravel road
Hiking One-Way/Total: 1.8/3.6 mi. *2.9/5.8 km* (Time 2/4 hours)
How Strenuous: Hard   *Total Drive & Hike Time:* 5 hrs/40 min.
Features: Alpine scenery, Vast views

NUTSHELL: A strenuous alpine hike up the north face of the San Francisco Peaks. The top of the trail was closed by an avalanche in 2005.

DIRECTIONS:
From Flagstaff City Hall (1) Go:
    North on Humphreys Street, 0.6 miles *1.0 km* to light. See Access Map, page 10. Turn left on Highway 180, the Grand Canyon road. At 19.0 miles *30.4 km* (MP 235.2) turn right on the upper Hart Prairie Road, FR 151 (2). At 20.6 miles *33.0 km*, turn left on FR 418 (3) and drive it to the 23.7 miles *37.9 km* point (4), where you will see a sign for the Bear Jaw and Abineau Trails. Turn right onto FR 9123-J and follow it to the 24.2 miles *38.7 km* point, where you fork left, then to the 24.3 miles *38.9 km* point, where you reach the parking loop.

TRAILHEAD: Above the parking lot, 35°23.183'N 111°40.619'W.

DESCRIPTION: From the trailhead you hike 0.4 miles *0.6 km* to a signed junction of the **Bear Jaw**/Abineau Trails, 35°22.978'N 111°40.407'W. Go right here.
    The trail climbs steadily, moving through a nice forest, the pitch getting ever steeper. You are in a canyon bottom, so there are no views out. From the 9,000 foot level, the forest is entirely spruce and the trail is very rocky and steep.
    At 1.8 miles *2.9 km* you break out into a clear area, and meet the avalanche, which is the stopping point until the avalanche damage is repaired. The official trail is 2.3 miles *3.7 km* long but the upper portion is now blocked. The view is breathtaking. Ahead of you (S), is the towering top of Mt. Humphreys, highest point in Arizona at 12,633 feet. Behind you (N), you can see forever.
    Before the avalanche the trail went up to a road, FR 146, and it was possible to turn left on the road and go east, downhill, for 2.1 miles *3.4 km* to the **Bear Jaw Trail** and go down it, making a 7.2 mile *11.5 km* loop.
    Even though the loop is temporarily out of service, the hike to the avalanche is well worthwhile.

Photo: This trail takes you up high on the San Francisco Peaks, through aspen forests, such as the one visible here.

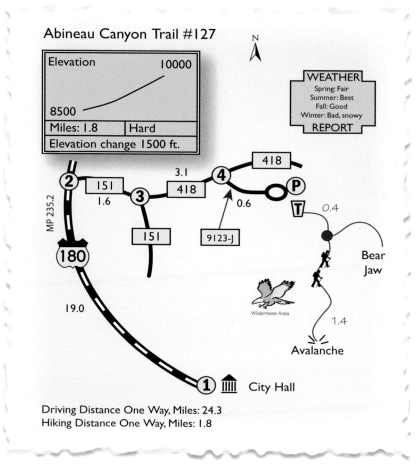

Abineau Canyon Trail #127

Elevation

10000

8500

| Miles: 1.8 | Hard |

Elevation change 1500 ft.

N

WEATHER
Spring: Fair
Summer: Best
Fall: Good
Winter: Bad, snowy
REPORT

418

2 — 151 — 3 — 418 — 4 — 418 — P

3.1

1.6

0.6

T 0.4

MP 235.2

151

9123-J

180

Bear Jaw

19.0

Wilderness Area

1.4

Avalanche

1 🏛 City Hall

Driving Distance One Way, Miles: 24.3
Hiking Distance One Way, Miles: 1.8

Anderson Mesa

Location Map E4
Lower Lake Mary USGS Map
Coconino Forest Service Map

Driving One-Way/Total: 13.5/27.0 mi. *21.6/43.2 km* (Time 25/50 minutes)
Access Road: All cars, All paved
Hiking One-Way/Total: 1.0/2.0 mi. *1.6/3.2 km* (Time 30/60 minutes)
How Strenuous: Easy   **Total Drive & Hike Time:** 1 hr. 50 min
Features: Easy to reach, Views

NUTSHELL: This hike takes you along a leg of The Arizona Trail to a scenic viewpoint.

DIRECTIONS:
From Flagstaff City Hall (1) Go:
    West, then south on Route 66 under the railroad overpass. At 0.5 miles *0.8 km*, leave Route 66 and go straight on Milton Road. See Access Map, page 10. At 1.7 miles *2.7 km* turn right at the light onto Forest Meadows Street. Go one block to Beulah. Turn left on Beulah and follow it south. Beulah merges onto Highway 89A. At 2.4 miles *3.8 km* (MP 401.6), turn left onto the Lake Mary Road (2). Follow the Lake Mary Road to the 12.0 miles *19.2 km* point (MP 334.3) (3) where you turn left on the paved Marshall Lake Road. Drive it to the 13.5 mile *21.6 km* point, the top of the mesa, taking the curve to the right toward the Lowell Observatory facility. There is a wide loop parking lot (cindered) to your left. Pull in here and park, 35°06.017'N, 111°32.192'W.

TRAILHEAD: Walk south across the entry road to an Arizona Trail marker, going through a log fence. This is the trailhead.

DESCRIPTION: The trail skirts the Lowell Observatory installation and brings you near Prime Lake (after pioneer George Prime). This lake is one of several lakes atop Anderson Mesa, and holds water only in a wet year.
    Soon after you leave the lake you head toward the edge of the mesa. Here you will see the typical Anderson Mesa landscape, with many shrubs and lots of open spaces. It is extremely rocky, with broken basalt lava rock all over the place. The rocks have been mostly cleared from the trail, so the walking is good.
    At a distance of 1.0 miles *1.6 km* we end this hike at a great viewpoint where the trail runs to the edge of a bare rock outcrop, 35°05.503'N, 111°31.967'W. You look down onto Lower Lake Mary. The dam at Upper Lake Mary is visible, plus a small part of that lake. Anderson Mesa is higher than the valley floor due to faulting. We stop at this viewpoint for a short but interesting day hike. You may want to wander back and forth along the rim in this area.

Photo: At the end of this trail, hikers look past volcanic cliffs to Lake Mary, a sweeping view.

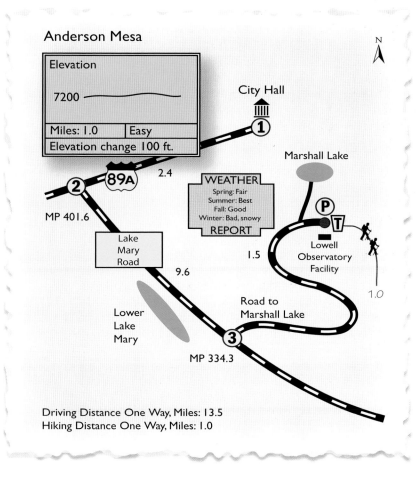

Anderson Mesa

N

Elevation

7200

| Miles: 1.0 | Easy |
| Elevation change 100 ft. | |

City Hall

1

89A   2.4

2

MP 401.6

Lake
Mary
Road

WEATHER
Spring: Fair
Summer: Best
Fall: Good
Winter: Bad, snowy
REPORT

Marshall Lake

P
T

Lowell
Observatory
Facility

1.5

9.6

Lower
Lake
Mary

Road to
Marshall Lake

1.0

3

MP 334.3

Driving Distance One Way, Miles: 13.5
Hiking Distance One Way, Miles: 1.0

Arizona Trail—Mormon Lake RR

Location Map F5
Mormon Lake & Mormon Mountain USGS Maps
Coconino Forest Service Map

Driving One-Way/Total: 24.9/49.8 mi. *39.8/79.7 km* (Time 30/60 minutes)
Access Road: All cars, Last 0.1 miles *0.2 km* good gravel road
Hiking One-Way/Total: 2.0/4.0 mi. *3.2/6.4 km* (Time 1.0/2.0 hours)
How Strenuous: Easy   *Total Drive & Hike Time:* 3 hours
Features: Historic logging railroad grade with ties

NUTSHELL: This portion of the Arizona Trail follows the grade of an old logging railroad near Mormon Lake.

DIRECTIONS:
From Flagstaff City Hall (1) Go:
    West, then south on Route 66 under the railroad overpass. At 0.5 miles *0.8 km*, leave Route 66 and go straight on Milton Road. See Access Map, page 10. At 1.7 miles *2.7 km* turn right at the light onto Forest Meadows Street. Go one block to Beulah. Turn left on Beulah and follow it south. Beulah merges onto Highway 89A. At 2.4 miles *3.8 km* (MP 401.6), turn left onto the Lake Mary Road (2). Follow the Lake Mary Road to the 23.0 mile *36.8 km* point (MP 323.6), where you turn right onto the Mormon Lake Road (Hwy 90) (3). At 24.8 miles *39.7 km*, turn right on FR 132 (4). Drive to the 24.9 mile *39.8 km* point, pull off the road wherever you can, and park, 34°59.006'N, 111°28.713'W.

TRAILHEAD: Walk down the road about 0.1 miles *0.16 km*. Turn right at the trail marker, 34°59.064'N, 111°28.790'W.

DESCRIPTION: There is no parking place—park where you can. We found a place to pull off as indicated above. The trail is easy to find and to follow.
    The trail runs parallel to an old logging railroad. This was originally the Arizona Mineral Belt, built in 1887. Later, in 1917, the Flagstaff Lumber Company used the old grade and put new ties and rails in place. The company logged until 1924, and then sold to Cady Lumber. The line was used for a few years, then discontinued. The costly rails were pulled up, but the cheap ties were left in place, making for a great ghost railroad. You will see places where the builders did an incredible amount of hand work, building elevated grades with dry-stacked stone.
    Other than the grade there is nothing exciting. The forest is very nice, but typical. We like to end the hike at the 2.0 mile *3.2 km* point, where there is a big elevated Vee, 34°00.309'N, 111°28.142'W. The trail runs on.

Photo: The old railroad bed here was a substantial one, with thousands of rocks stacked up to make a firm base. It's fun to follow it.

Arizona Trail—Mormon Lake Logging RR

N

Elevation

7200

Miles: 2.0	Easy
Elevation change 100 ft.	

City Hall

89A (US) 2.4

① City Hall

② MP 401.6

WEATHER
Spring: Fair
Summer: Best
Fall: Good
Winter: Bad, snowy
REPORT

Lake Mary Road

MP 323.6

20.6

③

Mormon Lake Road

2.0

1.8

T P ④ 0.1

132

Driving Distance One Way, Miles: 24.9
Hiking Distance One Way, Miles: 2.0

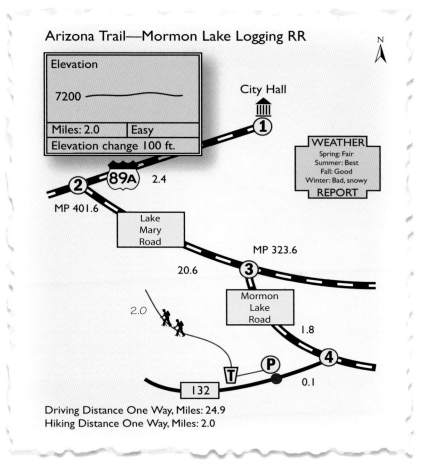

Beale Road—Laws Spring

Location Map D1
Sitgreaves Mountain and Squaw Mountain USGS Maps
Kaibab (Williams) Forest Service Map

Driving One-Way/Total: 36.8/73.6 mi. *58.9/117.8 km* (Time 1.0/2.0 hours)
Access Road: All cars, Last 10.3 miles *16.5 km* good gravel roads
Hiking One-Way/Total: 0.25/0.5 mi. *0.4/0.8 km* (Time 30/60 minutes)
How Strenuous: Easy   ***Total Drive & Hike Time:*** 3 hours
Features: Spring with petroglyphs, Historical 1850s wagon route

NUTSHELL: This hike takes you to an attractive historical site with an interpretive sign, rock art (both ancient and modern), and then onto the Beale Road.

DIRECTIONS:
From Flagstaff City Hall (1) Go:
    West a block on Route 66, then south, under the railroad. See Access Map, page 10. At 0.5 miles *0.8 km* turn right on Route 66. At 5.0 miles *8.0 km* merge onto I-40 West. At 23.7 miles *37.9 km* (MP 172) take Exit 171 for Pittman Valley (2). Turn left at the stop and take paved road FR 74 (Compressor Station). The paving ends at 26.5 miles *42.4 km*. At 31.4 miles *50.2 km* turn right on FR 141 (3). At 31.9 miles *51.0 km* turn left on FR 730 (4). At 34.1 miles *54.6 km* turn left on FR 115 (5). At 36.0 miles *57.6 km*, turn left on FR 2030 (Laws Spring sign). Drive to the parking lot at 36.8 miles *58.9 km.* 35°25.612'N, 112°03.925'W.

TRAILHEAD: Posted at the parking lot.

DESCRIPTION: Edward Beale blazed a government road across northern Arizona in 1857. The Beale Wagon Road was traveled heavily, then forgotten after the railroad came. Parts of the historic road have been located and marked.
    The trail takes you down a rocky path to a rock basin in a canyon. Look for ancient Indian rock art near the top. The reliable Laws Spring fills the basin with water, making it an important stop for travelers on the Beale Road. The words, "Laws Spring" were chiseled into a rock in 1859 by a member of Beale's crew. Look carefully and you will see other rock art, both ancient Indian and modern. The Forest Service has placed a nice explanatory plaque on the face of a boulder at the spring. 35°25.585'N, 112°03.998'W
    After you have enjoyed the spring, take the rest of the trail, up the other bank, a rocky but gentle climb. At the 0.25 mile *0.4 km* point, you will find a Beale Road marking post in a field 35°25.467'N, 112°03.947'W. This is officially the end of the hike, but you might want to walk part of the old road. Turn right at the marker and follow the cairns and posts as far as you wish.

Photo: This beautiful historic site contains some great rock art, such as the words, "Laws Spring" chiseled into the stone above the water.

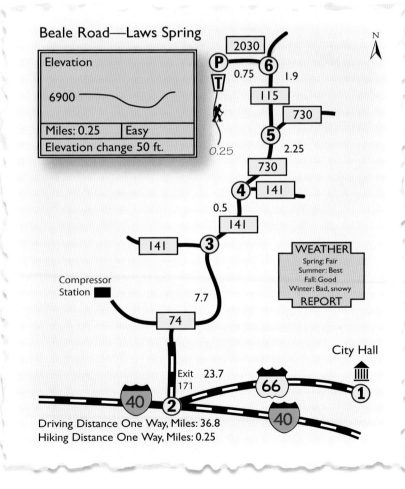

Beale Road—Laws Spring

Elevation

6900

Miles: 0.25	Easy
Elevation change 50 ft.	

2030

P T 0.75 6 1.9

115

730

5 2.25

0.25

730

4 141

0.5

141

141 3

Compressor Station

7.7

74

WEATHER
Spring: Fair
Summer: Best
Fall: Good
Winter: Bad, snowy
REPORT

City Hall

Exit 23.7
171

40 66 40

2 1

N

Driving Distance One Way, Miles: 36.8
Hiking Distance One Way, Miles: 0.25

Bear Jaw Canyon #26

Location Map C3
Humphreys Peak and White Horse Hills USGS Maps
Flagstaff Trails Map©

Driving One-Way/Total: 24.3/48.6 mi. *38.9/77.8 km* (Time 50/100 min.)
Access Road: All cars, Last 5.3 miles *8.5 km* gravel, in medium condition
Hiking One-Way/Total: 2.8/5.6 mi. *4.5/9.0 km* (Time 2.5/5.0 hours)
How Strenuous: Hard   ***Total Drive & Hike Time:*** 6 hours 40 min.
Features: Alpine scenery, Vast views

NUTSHELL: This is a strenuous hike up the north face of the San Francisco Peaks on an old sheep trail.

DIRECTIONS:
From Flagstaff City Hall (1) Go:
    North on Humphreys Street, 0.6 miles *1.0 km* to light. See Access Map, page 10. Turn left on Highway 180, the Grand Canyon road. At 19.0 miles *30.4 km* (MP 235.2) turn right on the upper Hart Prairie Road, FR 151 (2). At 20.6 miles *33.0 km*, turn left on FR 418 (3) and drive it to the 23.7 miles *37.9 km* point (4), where you will see a sign for the Bear Jaw and Abineau Trails. Turn right onto FR 9123-J and follow it to the 24.2 miles *38.7 km* point, where you fork left, then to the 24.3 miles *38.9 km* point, where you will reach the parking loop. Park at the parking lot.

TRAILHEAD: Above the parking lot, 35°23.183´N 111°40.619´W.

DESCRIPTION: From the trailhead you will hike a connector trail to a signed junction of the Bear Jaw/Abineau Trails in 0.4 miles *0.6 km.* 35°22.978´N 111°40.407´W. Go left there. (The **Abineau Canyon Trail** is closed at the top due to avalanche damage in the winter of 2004-2005).
    From the trail junction the Bear Jaw trail is fairly level, then dips a bit, and then starts to rise, getting steeper as it goes. It passes through beautiful woods, featuring heavy stands of aspens. You will pass through some old sheep camps, complete with herders' names carved on the aspen bark.
    You will climb through these woods for 2.8 miles *4.5 km*, to the end of the trail at the 9,700 foot point, where it meets Forest Road FR 146 35°22.240´N 111°38.803´W. Forest Road 146 is also known as the **Waterline Trail.**
    Before the avalanche closed the top of the Abineau Trail, hikers were able to make a loop by turning right on FR 146, hiking to the point where the Abineau Trail met FR 146, then hiking down Abineau to the Abineau/Bear Jaw trail junction, but until the avalanche damage is repaired, this is no longer permitted.

Photo: This trail takes you high on the north face of the San Francisco Peaks, through a beautiful forest. The trail is shored up here with a retaining wall.

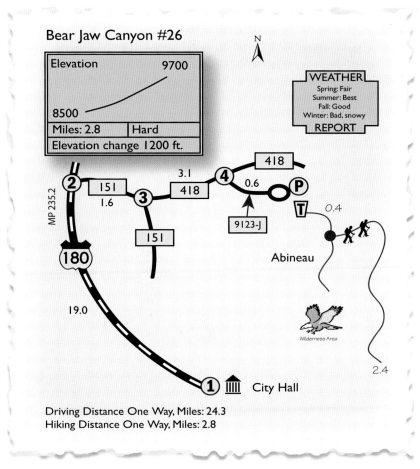

Bear Jaw Canyon #26

N

Elevation		9700
8500		
Miles: 2.8	Hard	
Elevation change 1200 ft.		

WEATHER
Spring: Fair
Summer: Best
Fall: Good
Winter: Bad, snowy
REPORT

MP 235.2

2 — 151 — 3 — 418 — 4 — 418
1.6   3.1   0.6

P
T   0.4

9123-J

180

19.0

Abineau

Wilderness Area

2.4

1 🏛 City Hall

Driving Distance One Way, Miles: 24.3
Hiking Distance One Way, Miles: 2.8

Benham Trail #38

Location Map D1
Williams South USGS Map
Kaibab (Williams District) Forest Service Map

Driving One-Way/Total: 36.0/72.0 mi. *57.6/115.2 km* (Time 1.0/2.0 hours)
Access Road: All cars, All paved except last 0.25 miles *0.4 km*
Hiking One-Way/Total: 4.5/9.0 mi. *7.2/14.4 km* (Time 2.75/5.5 hours)
How Strenuous: Hard   *Total Drive & Hike Time:* 7.5 hours
Features: Beautiful forest, High mountain, Views

NUTSHELL: This hike takes you up the east face to the top of Bill Williams Mountain outside the Town of Williams.

DIRECTIONS:
From Flagstaff City Hall (1) Go:
    South on Route 66 under the overpass. Turn right on Route 66 at the second light. See Access Map, page 10. At 5.0 miles *8.0 km* you will merge onto I-40 West. At 29.8 miles *47.7 km* take the Williams Exit, #165 (2). Go left at the stop sign to Williams and drive through town on Railroad Avenue to the 32.2 mile point *51.5 km* where you turn left on Fourth Street (3). As it leaves town its name changes to the Perkinsville Road (73). Stay on this road to the 35.8 miles *57.3 km* point, where you turn right onto the signed trail access road (4). Take this road to the 36.0 miles *57.6 km* point, the trail parking area.

TRAILHEAD: At the parking area 35°12.232'N, 112°10.372'W.

DESCRIPTION: It is hard to tell whether this trail was built as a road or as a pack trail. There are places where it is wide enough for a road, but the upper half looks only wide enough to have been a pack or foot trail. In any event, the trail was well engineered so that it climbs 1950 feet gradually.
    The trail goes up the east and south faces of the mountain. It does not get as much moisture as the **Bill Williams Mountain Trail** on the north side. Consequently, the forest is mostly pine with a lot of oak, until you reach aspen groves in the last mile *1.6 km*. There are some open areas for views, but generally the forest is heavy.
    At about the 1.5 mile *2.4 km* point you will enter into a gorgeous grove of oaks, really special. Mile posts have been inserted along the trail to mark your way. According to Dick's pedometer, they are accurate. You will cross the road, FR 111, five times as you go up the mountain. The fifth time is at the 4.0 mile *6.4 km* point, where the trail ends 35°11.965'N, 112°12.485'W. You can walk the road 0.5 miles *0.8 km* to the lookout tower, but don't count on being allowed inside.

Photo: One of the trails that goes up Bill Williams Mountain outside the town of Williams, this strenuous climb gives views out over a wide mountain area.

Benham Trail #38

Elevation	9250
7300	
Miles: 4.5	Hard
Elevation change 1950 ft.	

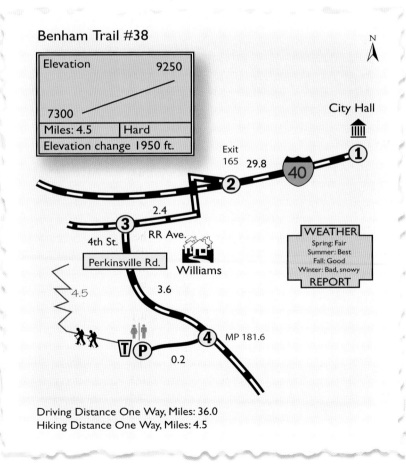

WEATHER
Spring: Fair
Summer: Best
Fall: Good
Winter: Bad, snowy
REPORT

City Hall

Exit 165   29.8

2.4

4th St.   RR Ave.

Perkinsville Rd.   Williams

4.5   3.6

MP 181.6

0.2

Driving Distance One Way, Miles: 36.0
Hiking Distance One Way, Miles: 4.5

Bill Williams Mtn. Trail #21

Location Map D1
Williams South USGS Map
Kaibab (Williams District) Forest Service Map

Driving One-Way/Total: 34.3/68.6 mi. *54.9/109.8 km* (Time 50/100 minutes)
Access Road: All cars, All paved
Hiking One-Way/Total: 4.4/8.8 mi. *7.0/14.1 km* (Time 3.0/6.0 hours)
How Strenuous: Hard   *Total Drive & Hike Time:* 7 hours 40 min.
Features: Beautiful forest, High mountain, Views

NUTSHELL: This hike takes you to the top of Bill Williams Mountain outside the Town of Williams.

DIRECTIONS:
From Flagstaff City Hall (1) Go:
    South on Route 66 under the overpass. Take Route 66 right at the second light. See Access Map, page 10. In 5.0 miles *8.0 km* you merge onto I-40 West. At 29.8 miles *47.7 km* take the Williams Exit, #165 (2). Drive through Williams on Railroad Avenue. Stay on the the street; do not return to I-40. At 33.4 miles *53.4 km*, turn left on Frontage Road (3). At 34.0 miles *54.4 km*, turn left on the road going to the Forest Service facility (4). Immediately after you turn, you will see a sign for the Bill Williams Mtn. Trail. Follow the sign. At the 34.3 mile *54.9 km* point pull into the parking lot.

TRAILHEAD: At the parking area. 35°14.255'N 112°12.888'W.

DESCRIPTION: At the trailhead you will see a large wooden map of trails on the mountain. The sign says that the Bill Williams Trail is 3.0 miles *4.8 km* long. We have found it to be longer than that. Whatever the true mileage, the trail is long, hard and steep.
    At 0.15 miles *0.2 km* you will come to the trail junction where the **Clover Spring Trail** takes off to the left 35°14.183'N, 112°12.752'W. At 0.9 miles *1.4 km* you will meet this trail again 35°13.973'N, 112°12.752'W. As you hike, you wind your way up through a nice pine forest. The trail climbs sharply and the forest changes character as you climb higher, becoming almost a rain forest, with lots of fir and spruce and aspens. The end of the **Bixler Saddle Trail** joins the trail at 35°12.135'N, 112°12.616'W, at the 3.5 mile *5.6 km* point.
    At 4.0 miles *6.4 km* the trail intersects FR 111, the road to the lookout tower. The forest prevents views until you reach this road, but from here up, the views are marvelous. You can quit here or hike the road 0.4 miles *0.6 km* up to the tower, but don't count on being allowed up into the tower.

Photo: If you like high mountain trails, then this one has plenty to offer. Some parts of the forest through which it winds are really lush, such as this one.

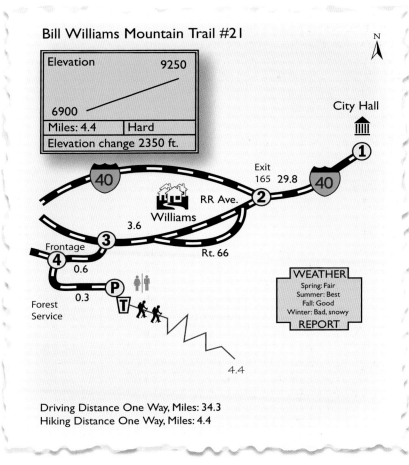

Bill Williams Mountain Trail #21

N

Elevation	9250
6900	
Miles: 4.4	Hard
Elevation change 2350 ft.	

City Hall

40

Exit
165 29.8

40

RR Ave.

Williams

3.6

2

Frontage

3

Rt. 66

4

0.6

P

0.3

T

Forest
Service

WEATHER
Spring: Fair
Summer: Best
Fall: Good
Winter: Bad, snowy
REPORT

4.4

Driving Distance One Way, Miles: 34.3
Hiking Distance One Way, Miles: 4.4

Bismarck Lake

Location Map C3
Humphreys Peak USGS Map
Flagstaff Trails Map©

Driving One-Way/Total: 16.6/33.2 mi. *26.6/53.1 km* (Time 40/80 minutes)
Access Road: All cars, Last 6.8 miles *10.9 km* good gravel roads
Hiking One-Way/Total: 1.0/2.0 miles *1.6/3.2 km* (Time 30/60 minutes)
How Strenuous: Moderate   *Total Drive & Hike Time:* 2 hours 20 min.
Features: Aspen groves, Mountain meadow, Sometime lake

NUTSHELL: You walk a former jeep road through an attractive mixed highland forest to an open meadow on the far side of which is an intermittent pond.

DIRECTIONS:
From Flagstaff City Hall (1) Go:
North on Humphreys St. 0.6 miles, *1.0 km* to a stoplight. See Access Map, page 10. Turn left onto Highway 180, the road to the Grand Canyon, and follow it out of town. At 9.8 miles *15.7 km* (MP 225.8), turn right onto FR 151, the lower Hart Prairie Road (2). Drive this gravel road to the 16.0 mile *25.6 km* point (3). Turn right on FR 627 and drive to the 16.6 mile *26.6 km* point, the fenced parking lot 35°21.811'N 111°44.065' W.

TRAILHEAD: Go through the gate at the parking area.

DESCRIPTION: You will walk old jeep roads that have been blocked so that motor vehicles can no longer drive them. The entire area is an elk preserve jointly sponsored by various benefactors as shown on the trailhead sign.
    The road makes a fine walking surface and you feel as if you are out in the remote countryside. Watch for game as you hike, as deer and elk are abundant in the preserve. Due to the elevation and other conditions, the forest though which you walk is very attractive, with a mixture of pine, spruce, fir, aspen and some lesser species. Ferns dot the woodside and there may be wildflowers.
    The trail rises gradually although the high elevation means that you may huff and puff a bit. Shortly beyond the midway point you climb up to an open shelf of open land where there is a large meadow covered with native grasses. The San Francisco Peaks are beautiful here, as you have a clear view of their west face. This is a good place in the autumn to see changing aspen leaves.
    You reach a trail junction at 35 21.795 N 111 43.428 W, where you go left. In a short distance you reach the lake at 35 21.842 N 111 43.307 W. We have seen the lake full of water in a wet year but most of the time it is a small pond. The area around it is one of great charm and we often just sit here and enjoy.

Photo: Calling this small pond a lake seems grandoise, but there is nothing petty about the scenery that surrounds it.

Bismarck Lake Trail

Elevation	8800
8550	
Miles: 1.0	Moderate
Elevation change 250 ft.	

N

WEATHER
Spring: Fair
Summer: Best
Fall: Good
Winter: Bad, snowy
REPORT

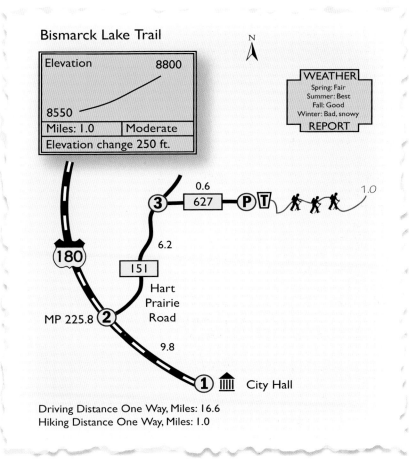

0.6

627

P T

1.0

180

6.2

151

Hart
Prairie
Road

MP 225.8 ②

9.8

① City Hall

Driving Distance One Way, Miles: 16.6
Hiking Distance One Way, Miles: 1.0

Bixler Saddle Trail #72

Location Map D1
McLellan Reservoir, Williams South USGS Maps
Kaibab (Chalender) Forest Service Map

Driving One-Way/Total: 42.9/85.8 mi. *68.6/137.3 km* (Time 1.0/2.0 hours)
Access Road: High clearance necessary for last 2.5 miles *4.0 km*
Hiking One-Way/Total: 2.5/5.0 mi. *4.0/8.0 km* (Time 1.5/3.0 hours)
How Strenuous: Hard   *Total Drive & Hike Time:* 5.0 hours
Features: Beautiful forest, Views, Great rock formations

NUTSHELL: This little-used trail takes you around the west face of Bill Williams Mountain.

DIRECTIONS:
From Flagstaff City Hall (1) Go:
   South on Route 66 under the railroad. See Access Map, page 10. Turn right at the light at 0.5 miles *0.8 km.* You will merge onto I-40 headed west at 5.0 miles *8.0 km.* Go past Williams, to the 37.9 mile *60.6 km* point, then take the Devil Dog Exit 157 (2). At the stop sign take the fork to the right and go south under I-40. You will come an intersection at 38.4 miles *61.4 km.* Take the left fork (S) (3). The paving ends soon at a cattle guard. You're now driving FR 108. At 38.8 miles *62.1 km* you come to a T junction (4). Turn left (E). At 39.2 miles *62.7 km* you reach a corner where the road ahead is blocked by a barrier. Turn right on FR 108 (5). At 39.3 miles *62.9 km* turn left (E) on FR 460 (6). At 40.4 miles *64.6 km* turn left on FR 45, the Bixler Saddle Road (7). The roads to this point have been fair, but FR 45 is very rough. Don't even try it if it is wet. You will drive it 2.5 miles *4.0 km* to the saddle, where you park, at 42.9 miles *68.6 km*, 35°11.884'N, 112°13.617'W.

TRAILHEAD: At the saddle.

DESCRIPTION: The trail heads northerly toward a gap between two immense, spectacular lava reefs, winding through a pretty forest of aspen, oak and fir. There are many viewpoints, some of which are quite breathtaking. From the 1.5 mile *2.4 km* point there are wonderful views to the south.
   After a long climb, the trail levels off and heads toward its end. Although the Forest Service rates this trail as 2.0 miles *3.2 km* long, we found it to be closer to 2.5 miles *4.0 km.* It ends in a heavy grove of fir and aspen where it intersects the **Bill Williams Mountain Trail**, 35°12.135'N, 112°12.616'W. From this junction the distance to the end of the Bill Williams Mountain Trail (a steep uphill climb) is 0.5 miles *0.8 km.*

Photo: This high mountain trail moves through tall lava cliffs. In places, such as this one, openings allows the hiker to gaze over miles of terrain.

Bixler Saddle Trail #72

Elevation	8740
7700	
Miles 2.5	Hard
Elevation change 1040 ft.	

WEATHER
Spring: Fair
Summer: Best
Fall: Good
Winter: Bad, snowy
REPORT

N

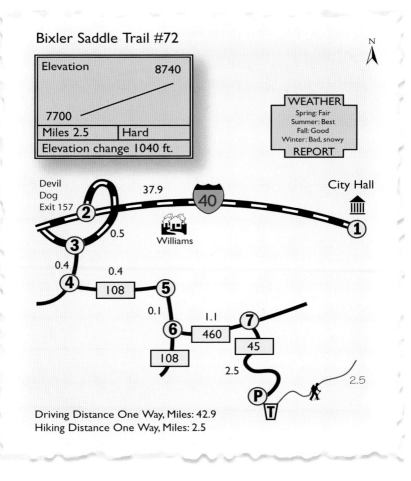

Devil
Dog
Exit 157 ② 37.9 40 City Hall ①
0.5 Williams
③
0.4 0.4
④ 108 ⑤
0.1 1.1
⑥ 460 ⑦
108 45
2.5 2.5
Ⓟ
Ⓣ

Driving Distance One Way, Miles: 42.9
Hiking Distance One Way, Miles: 2.5

Brookbank Trail #2

Location Map D3
Flagstaff West, Humphreys Peak & Sunset Crater West USGS Maps
Flagstaff Trails Map©

Driving One-Way/Total: 6.5/13.0 mi. *10.4/20.8 km* (Time 30/60 minutes)
Access Road: All cars, Last 1.0 miles *1.6 km* poor unpaved road
Hiking One-Way/Total: 3.2/6.4 mi. *5.1/10.2 km* (Time 2.0/4.0 hours)
How Strenuous: Hard   *Total Drive & Hike Time:* 5.0 hours
Features: Views, Forests

NUTSHELL: This trail starts on the Elden Lookout Road and winds around hills through scenic forests to join the **Sunset Trail** in the Mt. Elden trail system north of Flagstaff.

DIRECTIONS:
From Flagstaff City Hall (1) Go:
    North on Humphreys Street for 0.6 miles *1.0 km*. See Access Map, page 10. Turn left at the light onto Highway 180, the Grand Canyon Road. At 3.1 miles *5.0 km* (MP 218.6), turn right on the Schultz Pass Road, FR 420 (2). At the 3.6 mile *5.8 km* point go straight on the paved Elden Lookout Road (FR 557) (3). Follow FR 557 to the 6.5 mile *10.4 km* point, and then pull off to the left into an unmarked parking area and park, 35°15.474'N, 111°37.424'W.

TRAILHEAD: Walk up the road a few feet, and then you will see the trail sign on a closed road to your left.

DESCRIPTION: The trail goes up an old closed road that used to run to the Brookbank Ranch, passing through a beautiful alpine forest. You will see old rock work in several places, including some lines of rock that appear to be something other than roads. The trail eventually turns into a footpath. At 1.0 miles *1.6 km* you will reach a trail junction, 35°15.989'N, 111°37.860'W. The trail to the left goes uphill into private property in the Dry Lake Hills. Take the right fork.
    From the junction the trail makes a long arc to the north, winding around the shoulder of one of the hills. At the northernmost tip of the arc are good views of the San Francisco Peaks. Then you curve south, hiking through attractive forests of spruce and fir. The trail curves again, this time to the north.
    At 3.2 miles *5.1 km* the Brookbank Trail ends where it reaches a junction with the Sunset Trail, 35°16.109'N 111°36.662'W.
    To stay on the Brookbank Trail, you simply retrace your steps.

Photo: Although the trail starts in a typical Flagstaff pine forest, it rises through a beautiful mixed forest as it moves along.

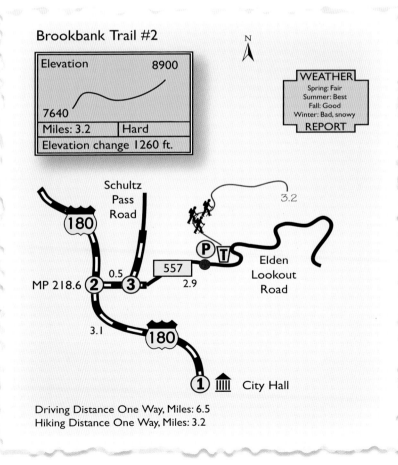

Brookbank Trail #2

N

Elevation   8900

7640

| Miles: 3.2 | Hard |

Elevation change 1260 ft.

WEATHER
Spring: Fair
Summer: Best
Fall: Good
Winter: Bad, snowy
REPORT

Schultz
Pass
Road

180

3.2

P T

0.5

557

2.9

Elden
Lookout
Road

MP 218.6 (2)——(3)

3.1

180

(1) 🏛 City Hall

Driving Distance One Way, Miles: 6.5
Hiking Distance One Way, Miles: 3.2

Buckskinner Trail #130

Location Map D1
Williams South USGS Map
Kaibab (Williams District) Forest Service Map

Driving One-Way/Total: 33.5/67.0 mi. *53.6/107.2 km* (Time 60/120 minutes)
Access Road: All cars, Last 0.5 miles *0.8 km* good gravel roads
Hiking One-Way/Total: 1.0/2.0 mi. *1.6/3.2 km* (Time 35/70 minutes)
How Strenuous: Moderate   *Total Drive & Hike Time:* 3 hours 10 min.
Features: Beautiful forest, Spring (usually dry)

NUTSHELL: This trail starts at Buckskinner Park and climbs through a nice mixed forest of pine and oak to Clover Spring.

DIRECTIONS:
From Flagstaff City Hall (1) Go:
    South on Route 66 under the overpass. Stay on Route 66 when it turns right at the second light. See Access Map, page 10. In 5.0 miles *8.0 km* you merge onto I-40 West. Drive I-40 to the 29.8 miles *47.7 km* point, then take Williams Exit, #165 (2). Go through Williams on Railroad Avenue to the 32.4 mile point *51.8 km* where you turn left on Seventh Street (3). Turn left on Route 66 (4). Turn right on Sixth Street (5). Drive to the end of Sixth Street and follow signs to Buckskinner Park, at 33.5 miles *53.6 km.*

TRAILHEAD: You will see a trailhead sign at the parking area, 35°14.151'N, 112°11.557'W.

DESCRIPTION: Buckskinner Park is a developed and maintained facility with picnic tables, toilet and other amenities. This allows the possibility of planning a picnic followed by a nice hike. You will see the turnoff and the picnic facilities clearly as you approach.
    From the picnic tables, the trail heads generally SW, up a gentle grade. Soon after the hike begins you will see what looks like a long wall through the trees. This was a water diversion weir constructed for city water storage purposes, and is no longer in use. After a climb of 0.6 miles *1.0 km* you will be on top of a knob and will see a canyon before you.
    You will hike part way down the canyon and then climb up again, moving laterally to get to Clover Spring 35°13.936'N, 112°12.229'W. We have been to Clover Spring several times and water was seldom running, and not much. Apparently this spring and many others in northern Arizona contained much more water in the old days than they do now. The spring has been captured in a concrete box. The water flows across the trail. This is the end of the **Clover Spring Trail.**

Photo: Although this is one of the tamer trails on Bill Williams Mountain, it does take you through some nice forest scenery.

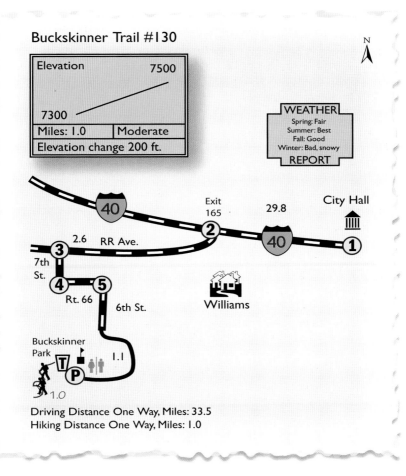

Buckskinner Trail #130

N

Elevation	7500
7300	
Miles: 1.0	Moderate
Elevation change 200 ft.	

WEATHER
Spring: Fair
Summer: Best
Fall: Good
Winter: Bad, snowy
REPORT

40

Exit 165

29.8

City Hall

②

2.6   RR Ave.

40

①

③ 7th St.

④ ⑤

Rt. 66   6th St.

Williams

Buckskinner Park

T P   1.1

1.0

Driving Distance One Way, Miles: 33.5
Hiking Distance One Way, Miles: 1.0

Buffalo Park Trails

Location Map D3
Flagstaff West USGS Map
Flagstaff Trails Map©

Driving One-Way/Total: 2.4/4.8 mi. *3.8/7.7 km* (Time 10/20 minutes)
Access Road: All cars, All paved
Hiking One-Way/Total: **Utility Access Trail** 0.5/1.0 mi. *0.8/1.6 km*; **Buffalo Park Urban Trail** 2.0 mi. *3.2 km* loop (Times 15/30 min. and 45 min.)
How Strenuous: Both are easy *Total Drive & Hike Times:* UA Trail 50 min. /BPU Trail 1 hr.
Features: Urban Trails, Easy to reach, Easy to walk

NUTSHELL: Buffalo Park is a beautiful grassy mesa, featuring well-maintained trails.

DIRECTIONS:
From Flagstaff City Hall (1) Go:
   North on Humphreys Street to the light at 0.6 miles *1.0 km* (2). See Access Map, page 10. Turn right onto Columbus Avenue and go one block east to Beaver Street (3). Turn left onto Beaver Street and go uphill. At the 1.1 mile *1.8 km* point turn right Forest Avenue at light (4). Drive Forest to the top of the hill. At 2.0 miles *3.2 km*, turn left on Gemini Drive (5). At 2.4 miles *3.8 km,* you will come to Buffalo Park. The parking lot is at 35°13.054'N 111°37.977'W.

TRAILHEADS: At the entrance arch.

DESCRIPTION: Utilities Access Trail: As you stand under the arch you will see this trail running straight north for 0.5 miles *0.8 km* to the fence marking the rear boundary of the park 35°13.523'N 111°37.855'W. At the end you will find a couple of metal buildings behind a chain link fence near the trail's end, where the trail veers to the northeast and you come to a gate where the **Oldham Trail No. 1** begins. This trail is the gateway to trails in the Mt. Elden trail system.
   Buffalo Park Urban Trail: This is the main trail, making a 2.0 mile *3.2 km* loop inside the park. We like to do the loop counterclockwise. Walk up the Utilities Trail about 100 yards, passing the **McMillan Mesa Trail**, and then take the next cindered path to your right (NE) 35°13.155'N 111°37.949'W. The trail will take you on a big wide wiggly loop around the mesa (see map).You will encounter fitness stations with placards and/or equipment describing some kind of exercise to be done on each spot. There are mileage markers every quarter mile, handy for runners.

Photo: This is a heavily used park inside the City of Flagstaff, but it has plenty of beautiful views, especially in summer when the fields are full of bloom.

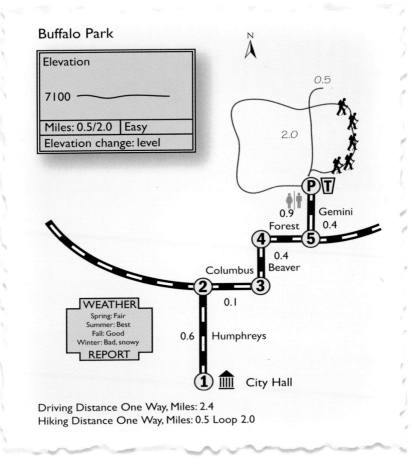

Buffalo Park

Elevation	
7100 ———————	
Miles: 0.5/2.0	Easy
Elevation change: level	

0.5

2.0

P **T**

0.9   Gemini
Forest   0.4

4 ———— **5**

0.4 Beaver

Columbus

2 ———— **3**

0.1

WEATHER
Spring: Fair
Summer: Best
Fall: Good
Winter: Bad, snowy
REPORT

0.6   Humphreys

1 🏛 City Hall

Driving Distance One Way, Miles: 2.4
Hiking Distance One Way, Miles: 0.5 Loop 2.0

Bull Basin Trail #40

Location Map C2
Kendrick Peak, Moritz Ridge and Wing Mt. USGS Maps
Kaibab Forest Service Map

Driving One-Way/Total: 35.0/70.0 mi. *56.0/112.0 km* (Time 1.25/2.5 hours)
Access Road: High clearance recommended for last few miles
Hiking One-Way/Total: 4.5/9.0 mi. *7.2/14.4 km* (Time 2.0/4.0 hours)
How Strenuous: Hard   *Total Drive & Hike Time:* 6.5 hours
Features: 10,418 foot peak, Views

NUTSHELL: This trail takes you up the north side of Kendrick Peak.

DIRECTIONS:
From Flagstaff City Hall (1) Go:
   North on Humphreys Street for 0.6 miles *1.0 km*. See Access Map, page 10. Turn left at the light onto Highway 180, the Grand Canyon Road. At 14.1 miles *22.6 km* (MP 230.1) (2) turn left onto gravel FR 245, and follow it to the 17.1 mile *27.4 km* point where it intersects FR 171 (3). Turn right on FR 171 and drive it to the 27.2 mile *43.5 km* point, where it meets FR 144 (4). Turn right on FR 144, taking it to the 28.7 mile *45.9 km* point (5). Turn right on FR 90 and drive it to the 34.4 mile *55.0 km* point (6). Turn right on FR 986 and follow it to the trail parking lot at 35.0 miles *56.0 km*.

TRAILHEAD: At the parking area, 35°26.233'N, 111°51.729'W.

DESCRIPTION: This area was devastated by a fire in 2000, requiring a new access road and a realignment of the trail. You no longer see Bull Basin. There is a map at the trailhead sign showing how the fire burned the mountain and explaining its mechanics and the role of fire in the forest ecosystem.
   You start hiking across a fire-damaged and eroded area. Be careful to follow the cairns, as the trail is hard to see in places. This trail gets little use so it is not well-worn. At 1.0 miles *1.6 km* is a trail junction where the Connector Trail goes to the right, 35°25.639'N, 111°51.904'W.
   Beyond it you begin to climb the mountain. The trail is well designed so that the grades are not too steep. The fire destroyed most of the fine forest that covered these slopes, making the hike less inviting, though it did open up viewing.
   At 3.0 miles *4.8 km* you will emerge onto a small saddle and follow a ridge line to the top. From here you hike through a boulder field. At 4.0 miles *6.4 km* you top out at the Old Ranger Cabin, built in 1911-1912, 35°24.476'N 111°51.009'W. It was protected from the fire and is in remarkably good shape. From the cabin it is another 0.5 miles *0.8 km* to the lookout tower.

Photo: This little-used trail on Kendrick Mountain moves through a forest that was heavily damaged in a forest fire, all too evident in this photo.

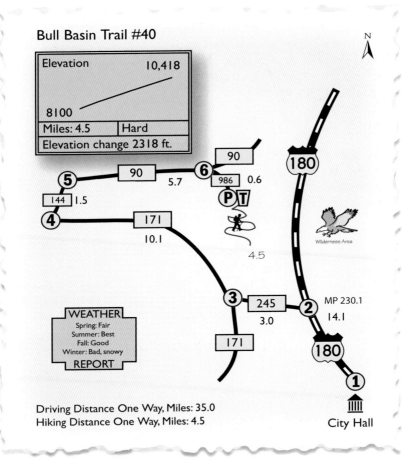

Bull Basin Trail #40

N

Elevation	10,418
8100	
Miles: 4.5	Hard
Elevation change 2318 ft.	

90

90

5.7

5

144 1.5

4

171

10.1

6

986 0.6

P T

4.5

180

Wilderness Area

3

245

3.0

2

MP 230.1

14.1

171

WEATHER

Spring: Fair
Summer: Best
Fall: Good
Winter: Bad, snowy

REPORT

180

1

City Hall

Driving Distance One Way, Miles: 35.0
Hiking Distance One Way, Miles: 4.5

Campbell Mesa Trails

Location Map D3
Flagstaff East USGS Map
Flagstaff Trails Map©

NEW

Driving One-Way/Total: 6.5/13 miles *10.4/20.8 km* (Time 10/20 minutes)
Access Road: All cars
Hiking Distances: Five loop trails of various lengths. See below
How Strenuous: All are Easy   *Total Drive & Hike Time:* Varies
Features: Convenient

NUTSHELL: This web of five loop trails offers a mix and match situation. The trails are a plain vanilla walk through the woods, nice but not exciting.

DIRECTIONS:
From Flagstaff City Hall (1) Go:
    East on Route 66. At 4.0 miles *6.4 km* turn right onto the freeway entrance ramp headed to Country Club Drive. Once on the ramp, don't take any of the exits. Keep going straight and you will merge onto Country Club Drive. At 5.6 miles *9.0 km* turn left on E. Old Walnut Canyon Road (2). At 6.5 miles *10.4 km* (3) turn left into the parking lot, in front of a steel gate, 35°11.991'N, 111°33.805'W.

TRAILHEAD: Walk up the road 0.1 mile *0.2 km*, 35°12.064'N, 111°33.665'W.

DESCRIPTION: The best way to understand this 5-trail network is to look at the map. The starting point for all the trails is the parking area described above.
    The distances of the trails, including the approaches, are as follows:
    Anasazi Loop: 2.8 miles *4.5 km*
    Campbell Mesa Loop: 5.0 miles *8.0 km*
    Continental Loop: 1.8 miles *2.9 km*
    Sinagua Loop: 1.3 miles *2.1 km*
    Walnut Meadows Loop: 3.8 miles *6.1 km*
    On the Walnut Meadows Loop there is a junction at 2.0 miles *3.2 km*, 35°10.962'N, 111°32.668'W where a connecting trail takes you across the Old Walnut Canyon Road to join the Arizona Trail.
    There are signposts at all of the necessary points, but we found that the mileage shown on these did not agree with our mileage. Don't worry about the discrepancies. We believe our mileage figures are correct.

Photo: The Campbell Mesa trails are not exciting but they do offer a variety of walks through Ponderosa pine forests near town.

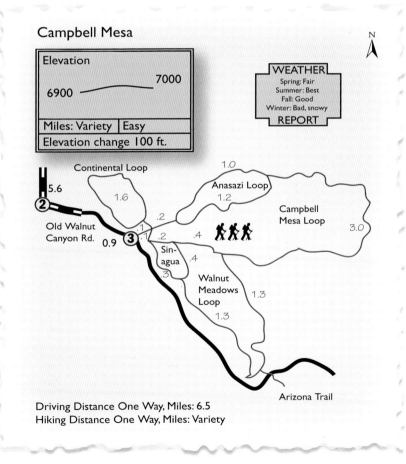

Campbell Mesa

Elevation	
6900 ⎯⎯⎯⎯⎯ 7000	
Miles: Variety	Easy
Elevation change 100 ft.	

WEATHER
Spring: Fair
Summer: Best
Fall: Good
Winter: Bad, snowy
REPORT

N

Continental Loop
1.0
Anasazi Loop
5.6
1.6
1.2
Campbell
Mesa Loop
.2
3.0
.1
Old Walnut
Canyon Rd. 0.9 .1 .2 .4
Sin-
agua .4
.3
Walnut
Meadows
Loop 1.3
1.3

Arizona Trail

Driving Distance One Way, Miles: 6.5
Hiking Distance One Way, Miles: Variety

Casner Mountain Trail

Location Map F2
Loy Butte, Sycamore Point USGS Maps
Coconino Forest Service Map

Driving One-Way/Total: 29.0/58.0 mi. *46.4/92.8 km* (Time 1.5/3.0 hours)
Access Road: High clearance only, Last 25.4 miles *40.6 km* unpaved, rough
Hiking One-Way/Total: 4.0/8.0 mi. *6.4/12.8 km* (Time 2.0/4.0 hours)
How Strenuous: Hard   ***Total Drive & Hike Time:*** 7 hours
Features: Views

NUTSHELL: Located 29.0 miles *46.4 km* southwest of Flagstaff, this hike follows the top of a ridge connecting Casner Mountain to the Mogollon Rim.

DIRECTIONS:
From Flagstaff City Hall (1) Go:
   West a block on Route 66, then south on Milton. See Access Map, page 10. At 0.5 miles *0.8 km* turn right on Route 66. At 2.6 miles *4.2 km* turn left on the Woody Mountain Road, FR 231 (2). It is paved about 1.0 mile *1.6 km,* then is a cinder road. At 16.6 miles *26.6 km* turn right on FR 538 (3). Drive it to the 26.1 mile *41.8 km* point, where you turn right on FR 538B as it branches off to the right (4) under a huge power line. The road is fair to the 28.25 mile *45.2 km* point but then becomes rough, with exposed rock. It ends at 29.0 miles *46.4 km,* on a ridge, where you park on a wide space to the right, 34°59.048'N, 111°56.629'W. Do not drive farther. If you reach the point where you can see the yellow road barrier, stop and back up to a place where you can turn around.

TRAILHEAD: At the parking place. You walk the road.

DESCRIPTION: The ridge you walk is so narrow that you can see off into the Sycamore side (right) or the Sedona side (left). Both are spectacular. It is mostly bare and unshaded and can be hot. At 0.25 miles *0.4 km* you come to a point where the Casner Mountain, Mooney and **Taylor Cabin** trails meet, 34°59.149'N, 111°56.774'W. Mooney goes left into the Sedona area. The Taylor Cabin Trail drops down into Sycamore Canyon on your right.
   The Casner Mountain Trail follows the contours of Buck Ridge as it dips and rises. At 2.5 miles *4.0 km* you dip into a saddle bottom. From there you begin the 1.0 mile *1.6 km*-long ascent that takes you onto Casner Mountain. You reach a bench on Casner at 3.5 miles *5.6 km* and then make the final push to the top (hike's end) at 4.0 miles *6.4 km.* 34°56.920'N, 111°59.122'W. The trail continues down the south face of Casner, a hike that is contained in our book, *Sedona Hikes.*

Photo: The character of this trail is clear from this photo: you walk out on an unshaded ridge, with tremendous views available to either side.

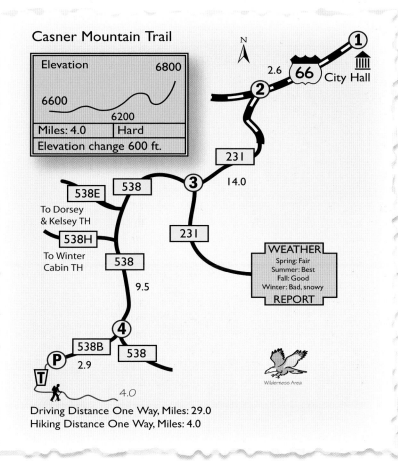

Casner Mountain Trail

N ↑

Elevation	6800
6600	
6200	
Miles: 4.0	Hard
Elevation change 600 ft.	

2.6 **66** City Hall

1

2

231

3 14.0

538E **538**

To Dorsey & Kelsey TH

538H

231

To Winter Cabin TH **538**

9.5

WEATHER
Spring: Fair
Summer: Best
Fall: Good
Winter: Bad, snowy
REPORT

4

P 538B **538**

2.9

Wilderness Area

4.0

Driving Distance One Way, Miles: 29.0
Hiking Distance One Way, Miles: 4.0

Christmas Tree Trail

Location Map D3
Flagstaff East USGS Map
Flagstaff Trails Map©

Driving One-Way/Total: 5.2/10.4 mi. *8.3/16.6 km* (Time 15/30 minutes)
Access Road: All cars, All paved
Hiking One-Way/Total: 2.0/4.0 mi. *3.2/6.4 km* (Time 1.0/2.0 hours)
How Strenuous: Moderate   *Total Drive & Hike Time:* 2½ hours
Features: Easy to reach, Pleasant forest

NUTSHELL: This trail is a connector between the **Fat Man's Loop** and the **Sandy Seep, Heart,** and **Little Elden-Heart** Trails. It is located at the base of Mt. Elden in East Flagstaff.

DIRECTIONS:
From Flagstaff City Hall (1) Go:
East, then north on Highway 89. See Access Map, pages 10-11. At 5.2 miles *8.3 km* (MP 419.5) just past the Flagstaff Mall, you will see a trailhead sign and a paved driveway to your left into a parking lot bounded by a pole fence (2). Pull in there and park, 35°13.812'N 111°34.762'W.

TRAILHEAD: At the parking area. You must hike the **Fat Man's Loop Trail** at first.

DESCRIPTION: From the parking lot, start off on the main trail. In 0.2 miles *0.3 km*, you will come to the Fat Man's Loop 35°14.178'N 111°34.888'W. Follow the sign and take the Fat Man's trail, to your right.

At the 0.5 mile *0.8 km* point, you will come to the Christmas Tree Trailhead. Turn right here. From this point, the Christmas Tree Trail runs along parallel to the base of Mt. Elden, heading generally north. It is easy to walk. There are many unofficial side trails but you should not have any trouble getting confused by these, as the main trail is easy to follow.

At 1.1 miles *1.8 km*, you will see a small concrete block building to your left, and a large earthen tank.

From this point, you have 0.9 miles *1.4 km* to go, intersecting the **Sandy Seep Trail** at the 2.0 mile *3.2 km* point 35°15.305'N 111°34.713'W. This is the end of the Christmas Tree Trail. The **Heart Trail** is 0.3 miles *0.5 km* ahead. The Christmas Tree Trail is not as scenic as the Fat Man's Loop, as you have no views, but it makes a welcome bit of variety and is useful as a connector.

Mountain bikers love the trails around Mt. Elden, including this one, so keep a lookout for them.

Photo: This hike provides a typical relaxing walk through the woods, along the base of Mt. Elden.

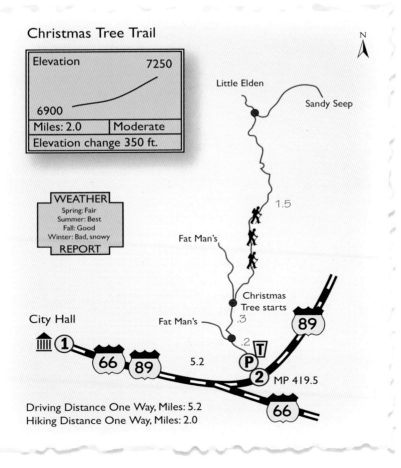

Christmas Tree Trail

N

Elevation 7250

6900

| Miles: 2.0 | Moderate |

Elevation change 350 ft.

WEATHER
Spring: Fair
Summer: Best
Fall: Good
Winter: Bad, snowy
REPORT

Little Elden

Sandy Seep

1.5

Fat Man's

Christmas
Tree starts
.3

City Hall

Fat Man's

.2

89

66 89

5.2

P T

2 MP 419.5

66

Driving Distance One Way, Miles: 5.2
Hiking Distance One Way, Miles: 2.0

Clover Spring Trail #46

Location Map D1
Williams South USGS Map
Kaibab Forest Service Map

Driving One-Way/Total: 34.3/68.6 mi. *54.9/109.8 km* (Time 50/100 minutes)
Access Road: All cars, All paved
Hiking One-Way/Total: 1.0/2.0 mi. *1.6/3.2 km* (Time 0.5/1.0 hour)
How Strenuous: Moderate   *Total Drive & Hike Time:* 2 hours 40 min.
Features: Beautiful forest, Views, Spring (usually dry)

NUTSHELL: This hike takes you through a nice forest to a spring on the flank of Bill Williams Mountain outside the Town of Williams.

DIRECTIONS:
From Flagstaff City Hall (1) Go:
   South on Route 66 under the overpass. Take Route 66 right at the second light. See Access Map, page 10. In 5.0 miles *8.0 km* you merge onto I-40 West. At 29.8 miles *47.7 km* take the Williams Exit, #165 (2). Drive through Williams on Railroad Avenue. Stay on the street; do not return to I-40. At 33.4 miles *53.4 km*, turn left, on Frontage Road (3). At 34.0 miles *54.4 km*, turn left on the road going to the Forest Service facility (4). As you enter the grounds you will see a sign for the Bill Williams Mountain Trail. Follow the sign. At 34.3 miles *54.9 km* is the parking lot.

TRAILHEAD: At the parking area 35°14.255'N, 112°12.888'W.

DESCRIPTION: You will hike along the Bill Williams Mountain Trail for a distance of 0.15 miles *0.2 km* to a trail junction, where you take the left fork for the Clover Spring Trail, 35°14.183'N, 112°12.752'W. At the 0.5 mile *0.8 km* point you come to another trail junction, 35°14.137'N, 112°12.453'W where the City of Williams Link Trail #124 peels off to the left. It goes 1.0 mile *1.6 km* to meet Sheridan Ave. just west of 11th Street in town. Stay on the Clover Spring Trail. The trail has had a low pitch up to this point. Soon it gets steeper for a short distance before leveling off again. At 0.9 miles *1.4 km* you come to the third trail junction to the right, a connector to the Bill Williams Trail, 35°13.983'N, 112°12.314'W. Go straight, and you will reach Clover Spring at the 1.0 mile *1.6 km* point, 35°13.936'N, 112°12.229'W. You will see the end of the **Buckskinner Trail** here.

   Clover Spring is disappointing. We have visited it a dozen times and found water there only twice. If you want to make a loop hike, going over to the Bill Williams Trail and coming down it, look at the map.

Photo: This is one of the shortest and easiest hikes on Bill Williams Mountain, but it has its places of interest.

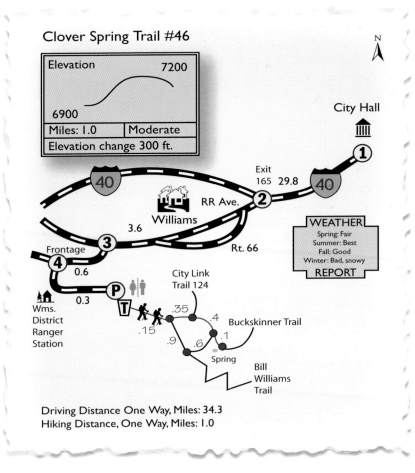

Clover Spring Trail #46

N

Elevation	7200
6900	
Miles: 1.0	Moderate
Elevation change 300 ft.	

City Hall

Exit
165 29.8

40

40

RR Ave.
Williams

3.6

2

WEATHER

Spring: Fair
Summer: Best
Fall: Good
Winter: Bad, snowy

REPORT

Frontage
3

Rt. 66

4

0.6

City Link
Trail 124

P

0.3

.35

.4   Buckskinner Trail

Wms.
District
Ranger
Station

.15

.9   .6   .1

Spring

Bill
Williams
Trail

Driving Distance One Way, Miles: 34.3
Hiking Distance, One Way, Miles: 1.0

Crystal Point Trail

Location Map F3
Munds Park & Mormon Mtn. USGS Maps
Coconino Forest Service Map

Driving One-Way/Total: 21.7/43.4 mi. *34.7/69.4 km* (Time 35/70 minutes)
Access Road: All cars, Last 0.2 miles *0.3 km* good gravel road
Hiking One-Way/Total: 1.5/3.0 mi. *2.4/4.8 km* (Time 40/80 minutes)
How Strenuous: Easy   *Total Drive & Hike Time:* 2½ hours
Features: Pleasant stroll through a pine forest

NUTSHELL: This hike is easy to reach on good roads.

DIRECTIONS:
From Flagstaff City Hall (1) Go:
    West, then south on Route 66 to Milton Road. See Access Map, page 10. Stay on Milton south as it turns into Interstate-17 (toward Phoenix). Drive I-17 south for 19.3 miles *30.9 km* and then take the Munds Park Exit 322 (2). Turn left at the stop sign. Drive through the Pinewood Subdivision on Pinewood Boulevard, the main road through the area. At 21.5 miles *34.4 km* you will reach a hilltop where the paved road ends, and a gravel road, FR 240, goes ahead into the forest. The Crystal Point trailhead is to the right, just before the paving ends. The parking area (3) is another 0.2 miles *0.3 km* farther, a big lot to your left, at 21.7 miles *34.7 km* 34°56.373'N, 111°37.191'W.

TRAILHEAD: At the point just before the paving ends 34°56.365'N, 111°37.344'W.

DESCRIPTION: The trail is 1.3 miles *2.1 km* long but you have to walk an additional 0.2 miles *0.3 km* to reach the trailhead. The trail moves along the top of a mesa in a southeasterly direction. Every now and then you get a glimpse through the trees, showing you that you are on a high ridge. The early going, up to the 1.0 mile *1.6 km* point is quite level and easy, moving through a typical pine forest. The trail is rocky all the way.
    The final segment of the trail moves more steeply uphill to the top of a knob, which is Crystal Point (though the USGS map does not give any name to the knob). Even on this last leg, the steepest part of the trail, the hike is not difficult, and the distance is short.
    The end of the trail is disappointing. It ends at a good viewpoint but the tree cover is so heavy that the views are restricted. There is a picnic table and an ammo can containing log books. Some wag has rigged up an electric coffee pot "plugged in" to an imaginary outlet. The trail ends at 34°55.837'N, 111°36.512'W.

Photo: Dick is taking it easy at the end of the trail, though the trail will not tire you.

Crystal Point Trail

N

Elevation	7190
6800	
Miles: 1.5	Easy
Elevation change 390 ft.	

City Hall

1

WEATHER
Spring: Fair
Summer: Best
Fall: Good
Winter: Bad, snowy
REPORT

19.5 mi. 17

Exit 322
Munds Park 2
Pinewood

2.2

P

240

3

T

Pinewood Blvd.

1.5

Driving Distance One Way, Miles: 21.7
Hiking Distance One Way, Miles: 1.5

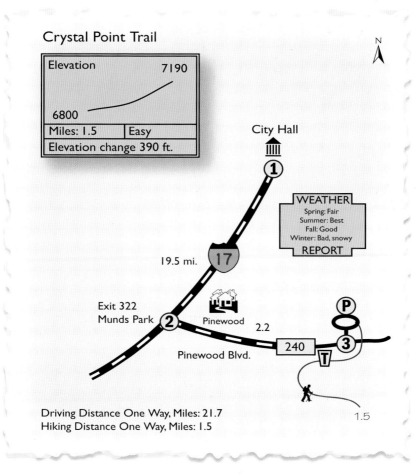

Davenport Hill Trail #63

Location Map D1
Williams South & Davenport Hill USGS Maps
Kaibab (Williams District) Forest Service Map

Driving One-Way/Total: 39.9/79.8 mi. *63.8/127.7 km* (Time 1.0/2.0 hours)
Access Road: All cars, Last 4.0 miles *6.4 km* good gravel road
*Hiking One-Way/Total:*2.5/5.0 mi. *4.0/8.0 km* (Time 1.25/2.5 hours)
How Strenuous: Moderate   *Total Drive & Hike Time:* 4.5 hours
Features: Beautiful forest, Lake, Views

NUTSHELL: Starting at pretty Dogtown Lake, this trail moves through a pine forest and then climbs to the top of a hill.

DIRECTIONS:
From Flagstaff City Hall (1) Go:
   South on Route 66 through the overpass. Take Route 66 right at the second stoplight. See Access Map, page 10. In 5.0 miles *8.0 km* merge onto I-40 West. At 29.8 miles *47.7 km*, take the Williams Exit, #165 (2). Go left into Williams on Railroad Ave. and at 32.2 miles *51.5 km* turn left on Fourth Street (3), the Perkinsville Rd (Hwy 73). At 35.9 miles *57.4 km*, turn left onto FR 140 (4). (Sign: "Dogtown Lake"). At 38.7 miles *61.9 km*, turn left on FR 132 (5) and drive into Dogtown CG. Follow signs to the boat ramp and park in the lot.

TRAILHEAD: At the parking area, 35°12.701'N, 112°07.506'W.

DESCRIPTION: At the parking area you will see a sign for the Ponderosa Trail, a self-guided nature trail. Affixed to the signpost is a dispenser containing a trail brochure which explains what you will see at 13 stations along the trail. Hike the Ponderosa Trail to station #6. Turn right here. You will reach station #12 in a few steps. Keep going until you come to station #10, where the Davenport Hill Trail begins, 35°12.931'N, 112°07.343'W.
   The trail moves northeasterly and makes a gradual climb. The trail crosses a forest road at about 1.0 miles *1.6 km*, 35°13.259'N, 112°06.495'W.
   You are at the foot of Davenport Hill and begin to climb it, a much steeper section of the trail. The trail winds back and forth, which gives you different viewpoints, though the forest is so thick that you only get glimpses outward. You reach an intermediate top at 1.5 miles *2.4 km*, a good resting point, and then begin the final ascent. Toward the top you hike through a dense forest of oak, pine, fir and spruce, really lovely. The trail takes you up to the farthest point on the hill where it stops at a large cairn. There is a sign here reading, "Davenport Hill, Elevation 7805", 35°13.410'N, 112°05.853'W.

Photo: This hike in the Williams area enjoys a variety of scenery, winding through a Ponderosa pine forest to Davenport Hill, which it climbs.

Davenport Hill Trail #63

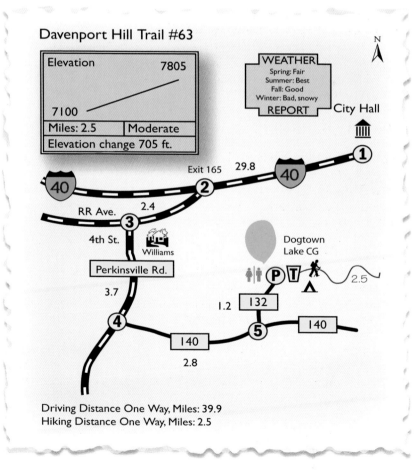

Elevation	7805
7100	
Miles: 2.5	Moderate
Elevation change 705 ft.	

WEATHER
Spring: Fair
Summer: Best
Fall: Good
Winter: Bad, snowy
REPORT

City Hall

N

City Hall

Exit 165   29.8

40

40

2

1

RR Ave.   2.4

3

4th St.

Williams

Dogtown
Lake CG

Perkinsville Rd.

P   T

2.5

3.7

1.2   132

4

140

5

140

2.8

Driving Distance One Way, Miles: 39.9
Hiking Distance One Way, Miles: 2.5

Deer Hill Trail

Location Map D4
Sunset Crater West USGS Map
Coconino Forest Service Map

Driving One-Way/Total: 11.7/23.4 mi. *18.7/37.4 km* (Time 30/60 minutes)
Access Road: All cars, Last 2.5 miles *4.0 km* good gravel road
Hiking One-Way/Total: 5.3/10.6 mi. *8.5/17.0 km* (Time 3.0/6.0 hours)
How Strenuous: Hard (due to length)   *Total Drive & Hike Time:* 7 hours
Features: Forests, Old logging railroad beds, Close to town

NUTSHELL: This trail runs from the Little Elden Horse Camp to a point off the Schultz Pass Road, at times running atop old logging RR grades.

DIRECTIONS:
From Flagstaff City Hall (1) Go:
    East, then north on Highway 89. See Access Map, pages 10-11. Take Highway 89 to the 9.2 mile *14.7 km* point (MP 423.3) (2) where you turn left on the gravel Elden Spring Road, FR 556. Drive to the 11.7 miles *18.7 km* point, where you turn right into a parking lot 35°16.131'N, 111°36.420'W (3). Do not drive directly into the Horse Camp, as that is for equestrians only.

TRAILHEAD: North end of the Horse Camp. 35°16.872'N, 111°34.651'W.

DESCRIPTION: From the parking area hike 0.6 miles *1.0 km* to the Horse Camp following the signs. Pass through the camp gate and walk in, turning left at the first red gravel road and walking to the top (N) end of the camp, looking for Space #13. Northwest of this space the trail goes into the woods.
    At 0.7 miles *1.1 km* you pass through a yellow gate and hike along a fence to your right (W), then at 0.85 mi. *1.4 km* you turn right (N), still following the fence. This fence runs along the section lines due north and you will follow it all the way. At 1.0 miles *1.6 km* you will see two giant water tanks to your left.
    At 1.1 miles 1.*8 km* you cross a road and pipeline. Don't go through the blue fence or over the cattle guard. Soon the trail dips into Weatherford Canyon, rises, then crosses a wash. Here you are walking along the flank of Deer Hill, which rises above to your left. You will hold the same contour line pretty steadily until the end. You will pass through two gates, moving off Deer Hill at the second one. Shortly beyond, where the path curves around a wash, you will briefly be walking on the bed of the 1896-1925 Greenlaw logging railroad. At a later point you will be on another bit of the railroad grade, easier to see because of the rock work, 35°19.784'N, 111°34.753'W. At the end the trail opens a bit for views, then climbs to a point off the Schultz Pass Road 35°20.678'N, 111°34.525'W.

Photo: Deer Hill itself is sensed rather than seen because of the heavy tree cover, but there are open meadows such as this one to add scenic interest.

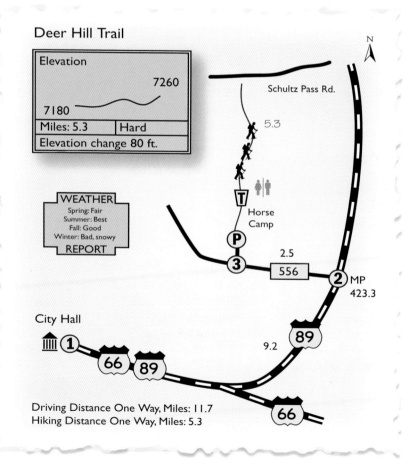

Deer Hill Trail

Elevation	
7260	
7180	
Miles: 5.3	Hard
Elevation change 80 ft.	

WEATHER
Spring: Fair
Summer: Best
Fall: Good
Winter: Bad, snowy
REPORT

Schultz Pass Rd.

5.3

Horse Camp

2.5
556

MP
423.3

City Hall

89

66 89

9.2

66

Driving Distance One Way, Miles: 11.7
Hiking Distance One Way, Miles: 5.3

Doney Trail #39

Location Map C4
Wupatki SW USGS Map
Coconino Forest Service Map

Driving One-Way/Total: 42.0/84.0 mi. *67.2/134.4 km* (Time 1.0/2.0 hours)
Access Road: All cars, All paved
Hiking One-Way/Total: 0.7/1.4 mi. *1.1/2.2 km* (Time 20/40 minutes)
How Strenuous: Moderate   *Total Drive & Hike Time:* 2 hours 40 min.
Features: Views, Indian ruins

NUTSHELL: Located in the Wupatki National Monument area this trail takes you to the top of two cinder cones for nice views.

DIRECTIONS:
From Flagstaff City Hall (1) Go:
   East, curving to north on Highway 89. See Access Map, pages 10-11. At 16.4 miles *26.2 km* (MP 430.3) turn right at the entrance to Sunset Crater National Monument (2). At 18.4 miles *29.4 km* stop at the ticket booth to pay admission. Just beyond that is the Sunset Crater Visitor Center, which is worth a look.
   At 26.0 miles *41.6 km* you reach the Painted Desert Vista—worth a side trip to enjoy the view. At 37.8 miles *60.5 km* you reach the road to the Wupatki Visitor Center to your left—worth a detour for a look. Stay on the main road to the 41.9 mile *67.0 km* point, where you turn left into the Doney Picnic Ground (3). At 42.0 miles *67.2 km* you will reach the parking area, 35°31.906'N 111°24.243'W.

TRAILHEAD: At the parking area.

DESCRIPTION: The trail leads to a saddle between two cinder cones at 0.1 miles *0.2 km*, 35°31.812'N, 111°24.260'W. Go left first, to the lower cone. It's 0.1 miles *0.2 km* to the top, a climb of 100 feet. You will see some informative signs along the path. Near the top is a small, crude Indian ruin. There are good views from the top, 35°31.847'N, 111°24.230'W.
   Then it's back down to the saddle and 0.5 miles *0.8 km* up the higher cone. You will find a small partially excavated pit house on the way. At the top is a bench where you can sit and enjoy the views. There is a nice sign with a sketch identifying the mountains you see to the west, 35°31.648'N, 111°24.384'W. Interpretive signs have been placed at several stations along the trail, adding to the enjoyment of this pleasant hike.
   Because these tops are bare cinder cones your view is unobstructed and you can see for miles. Ben Doney believed that there was treasure buried in these hills and spent years in a fruitless search for it.

Photo: Dick is just beyond the saddle, heading up to the top of one of the craters. Views of the Painted Desert and San Francisco Peaks are spectacular.

Doney Trail #39

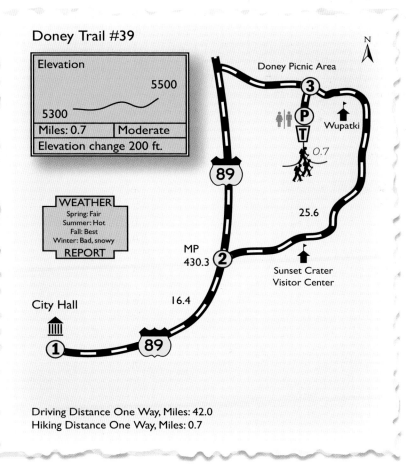

Elevation	
	5500
5300	
Miles: 0.7	Moderate
Elevation change 200 ft.	

WEATHER
Spring: Fair
Summer: Hot
Fall: Best
Winter: Bad, snowy
REPORT

N

Doney Picnic Area

3

Wupatki

0.7

89

25.6

MP
430.3 **2**

Sunset Crater
Visitor Center

City Hall

16.4

1 **89**

Driving Distance One Way, Miles: 42.0
Hiking Distance One Way, Miles: 0.7

Dorsey Spring Trail #7

Location Map F2
Sycamore Point USGS Map
Coconino Forest Service Map

Driving One-Way/Total: 23.0/46.0 mi. *36.8/73.6 km* (Time 1.0/2.0 hours)
Access Road: High clearance needed last 0.7 miles *1.1 km*
Hiking One-Way/Total: 2.8/5.6 mi. *4.5/9.0 km* (Time 1½/3.0 hours)
How Strenuous: Hard   ***Total Drive & Hike Time:*** 5 hours
Features: Hidden spring, Virgin forests

NUTSHELL: Located 23.0 miles *36.8 km* southwest of Flagstaff, this trail takes you part of the way into Sycamore Canyon to a beautiful spring.

DIRECTIONS:
From Flagstaff City Hall (1) Go:
   West a block on Route 66, then south, through the railroad overpass. See Access Map, page 10. At 0.5 miles *0.8 km* turn right on Route 66. At 2.6 miles *4.2 km* turn left on the Woody Mountain Rd, FR 231 (2). At 16.6 miles *26.6 km* turn right on FR 538 (3). At 22.3 miles *35.7 km* turn right on FR 538E (4). At 22.7 miles *36.3 km* turn left on FR 538E (5). Drive to the 23.0 mile *36.8 km* point and park, 35°03.545'N, 111°55.032'W. Note: The road from Dorsey Spring TH to Kelsey Spring TH has been deteriorating for years. When we tested it in November 2006 it was so bad that it is dangerous so we have deleted the hikes originating from the Kelsey Spring TH.

TRAILHEAD: At the parking area. It is signed.

DESCRIPTION: The Dorsey Spring Trail does not start at the rim of Sycamore Canyon. You begin by walking a closed road. At 0.25 miles *0.4 km* you reach the Hog Hill #70A trailhead (we omit this trail, as we think it not worthwhile). At 2.0 miles 3.2 *km* you reach the rim. You get a few views into the depths of the canyon, but views into Sycamore Canyon are scarce on this trail.
   You hike down into Sycamore along a side canyon. It is fairly steep and the footing is tricky in places but you only have to go 0.8 miles 1.3 *km*, to the spring. The spring is to your left, 35°03.255'N, 111°56.736'W. The water flows from a black plastic pipe into a small pool. The spring is usually dependable but the water should be treated before drinking due to the threat of giardia.
   Dorsey Spring is located about midway between Kelsey Spring and Winter Cabin on the **Kelsey-Winter Trail.** You can go north along Kelsey-Winter about 2.0 miles *3.2 km* to Babe's Hole and into the gorge of Sycamore Canyon via Little LO trail or you can go south about 2.0 miles *3.2 km* to **Winter Cabin.**

Photo: Sherry is refreshing herself by dipping her hand in the waters of this reliable spring, hidden in a remote glade in the Sycamore Canyon area.

Dorsey Spring Trail #7

Elevation	
6950	
	6200
Miles: 2.8	Hard
Elevation change 750 ft.	

N

WEATHER
Spring: Fair
Summer: Best
Fall: Good
Winter: Bad, snowy
REPORT

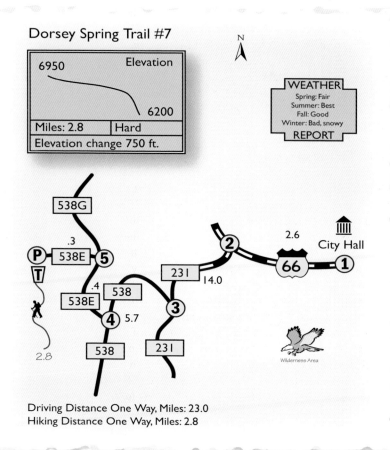

538G

.3
P 538E 5
T

2.6
2 City Hall
66 1

231 14.0

.4
538
538E
3
4 5.7

2.8

538 231

Wilderness Area

Driving Distance One Way, Miles: 23.0
Hiking Distance One Way, Miles: 2.8

Elden Lookout Trail #4

Location Map D4
Flagstaff East USGS Map
Flagstaff Trails Map©

Driving One-Way/Total: 5.2/10.4 mi. *8.3/16.6 km* (Time 10/20 minutes)
Access Road: All cars, All paved
Hiking One-Way/Total: 2.5/5.0 mi. *4.0/8.0 km* (Time 2.0/4.0 hours)
How Strenuous: Hard   *Total Drive & Hike Time:* 4 hours 20 min.
Features: Views

NUTSHELL: This steep rocky trail runs from the base of Mt. Elden in East Flagstaff to a fire lookout tower at the top of the mountain.

DIRECTIONS:
From Flagstaff City Hall (1) Go:
    East, then north on Highway 89. See Access Map, pages 10-11. At 5.2 miles *8.3 km* (MP 419.5) just past the Flagstaff Mall, you will see a trailhead sign and a paved driveway to your left into a parking lot bounded by a pole fence (2). Pull in there and park. 35°13.812'N 111°34.762'W.

TRAILHEAD: At the parking lot.

DESCRIPTION: At the start this trail is the same as the **Fat Man's Loop Trail,** which branches to the right at 0.2 miles *0.3 km* 35°13.398'N 111°34.913'W. You will see clearly by now that you are walking directly toward Mt. Elden, climbing gradually. At the 0.5 miles *0.8 km* you will reach the junction with the **Pipeline Trail**, which goes left 35°14.058'N 111°35.102'W. As you near the mountain the trail becomes much steeper. At 0.9 miles *1.4 km* you reach a junction with the Fat Man's Loop, where a sign shows the Elden Lookout Trail going uphill 35°14.367'N 111°35.102'W.
    From this point to the top, 1.4 miles *2.2 km*, the trail is very steep. There is hardly a level stretch anywhere. The trail was built in 1914 so rangers could get to the tower. In some places "stairs" have been built and in others cribbing has been used to hang the trail out over space.
    The forest through which you pass on your way to the top is not heavy. This is due to the terrain and a 1977 forest fire. Consequently there are many open spaces for great views.
    The trail struggles to the top at the 2.3 mile *3.7 km* point, below the fire tower 35°14.582'N 111°35.716'W. It is another is 0.2 miles *0.3 km* up to the tower. If you have enough energy, by all means, make this final ascent, because the views at the top are as good as any in the Flagstaff area.

Photo: You're on top of the world here...or at least on top of Mt. Elden. The sparse tree growth at the end of the trail allows you to see forever.

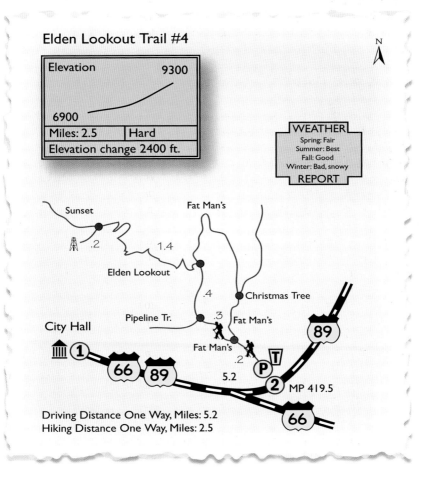

Elden Lookout Trail #4

N

Elevation	9300
6900	
Miles: 2.5	Hard
Elevation change 2400 ft.	

WEATHER
Spring: Fair
Summer: Best
Fall: Good
Winter: Bad, snowy
REPORT

Sunset

.2

1.4

Fat Man's

Elden Lookout

.4

Christmas Tree

Pipeline Tr.

.3 Fat Man's

City Hall

1

Fat Man's

.2

66 89

5.2

P T

89

2 MP 419.5

66

Driving Distance One Way, Miles: 5.2
Hiking Distance One Way, Miles: 2.5

Elden Pueblo

Location Map D4
Flagstaff East USGS Map
Coconino Forest Map

Driving One-Way/Total: 6.4/12.8 mi. *10.2/20.5 km* (Time 10/20 minutes)
Access Road: All cars, All paved
Hiking One-Way/Total: 0.1/0.2 mi. *0.2/0.3 km* (Time 10/20 minutes)
How Strenuous: Easy   *Total Drive & Hike Time:* 40 minutes
Features: Indian ruins located inside Flagstaff city limits

NUTSHELL: Interesting Indian ruins, presently being excavated. Located just north of Flagstaff, this is more of a sightseeing excursion than a hike, as you do very little walking.

DIRECTIONS:
From Flagstaff City Hall (1) Go:
    East, then north on Highway 89. See Access Map, pages 10-11. At 6.4 miles *10.2 km* (MP 420.7), you will see a sign, "Elden Pueblo Ruins" and a gravel drive going into the trees to your left just before the stoplight at the junction of Highway 89 and the Townsend-Winona Road (2). This is the entrance to the parking area for Elden Pueblo. Pull in there and park.

TRAILHEAD: There are no trail signs. A path starts at the west end of the parking lot, 35°14.636'N 111°34.032'W.

DESCRIPTION: The Elden Pueblo ruins are undergoing restoration but this is sporadic and there is no way of knowing on any particular day whether anyone will be there. If no one is present, you are welcome to help yourself and wander around. Unfortunately there are no self-guiding signs. The footpaths are clearly marked by stone borders. Just wander around on the paths and enjoy looking.
    Elden Pueblo was discovered in October 1916 by Mary-Russell Ferrell Colton, while horseback riding. The prominent federal archaeologist Jesse Fewkes conducted digs at the site in 1926 and sent carloads of artifacts from Elden Pueblo to the Smithsonian. The dismay of townspeople at seeing this wholesale loss of local relics was one of the main reasons that Mrs. Colton and her husband joined other townspeople and organized the Museum of Northern Arizona.
    A look at this site shows you how much effort goes into excavation. You can appreciate better what has happened at some fully restored places such as Wupatki or Tuzigoot when you look at the work here. The more they dig at Elden Pueblo, the bigger the ruin seems and additional discoveries are made.

Photo: There's not much hiking here, but there is plenty to see. This is one of the few places anywhere that allow the public to have free access to ruins.

Elden Pueblo

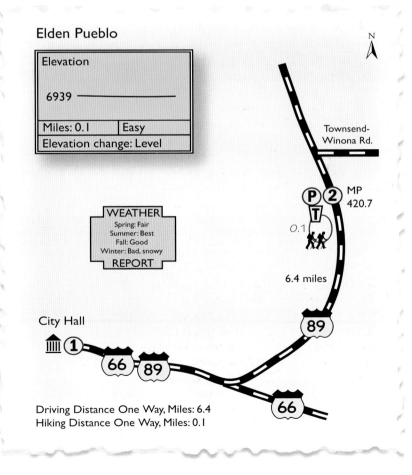

Elevation	
6939 ————————	
Miles: 0.1	Easy
Elevation change: Level	

WEATHER
Spring: Fair
Summer: Best
Fall: Good
Winter: Bad, snowy
REPORT

Townsend-
Winona Rd.

P 2 MP
T 420.7

0.1

6.4 miles

89

City Hall

66 89

66

Driving Distance One Way, Miles: 6.4
Hiking Distance One Way, Miles: 0.1

Elden Spring Loop

Location Map D4
Flagstaff East USGS Map
Coconino Forest Service Map

Driving One-Way/Total: 5.1/10.2 mi. *8.2/16.3 km* (Time 20/40 minutes)
Access Road: All cars, All paved
Hiking Distance, Complete Loop: 2.5 miles *4.0 km* (Time 1.0 hour 20 min.)
How Strenuous: Moderate   *Total Drive & Hike Time:* 2 hours
Features: Historic homesite and grave, Great lava cliffs and boulders, Spring

NUTSHELL: A short drive takes you to this trail that packs many features into a loop. This is a good one for kids.

DIRECTIONS:
From Flagstaff City Hall (1) Go:
    East, then north on Highway 89. See Access Map, pages 10-11. At 4.6 miles *7.4 km* (just before you arrive at the Flagstaff Mall) turn left on Cummings (Pizza Hut on the corner) (2). Go up Cummings to its end, by Christensen School, and turn left on El Paso at 4.8 miles *7.7 km* (3). Drive out El Paso for four blocks to Hamblin. Here you will see a wide unpaved apron to the right. Pull off on it and drive up to the pipeline fence, where you see a wide white gate flanked by two big H posts, at 5.1 miles *8.2 km*. Park at the gate, 35°13.577'N, 111°35.400'W.

TRAILHEAD: There are no trail signs where you park. Step over the criss-crossed logs that serve as a gate and go up the pipeline road.

DESCRIPTION: Walk the road to the top of the hill, where at 0.25 miles *0.4 km*, you turn on a footpath to the right (N), (sign about the Mt. Elden Environmental Study Area) 35°13.565'N, 111°35.626'W.
    There are many trails, including abandoned nature trails. Stay on the main trail. Soon you come to a trail junction. Go left. At 0.6 miles *1.0 km*, you will come to a clearing where you will see trail signs and a sign for the Elden Homesite, 35°13.652'N, 111°36.089'W. Toward Mt. Elden (N) is a rough path down into a gully. This goes to Elden Spring, a short detour, and worth seeing.
    Next, walk west on the main path. Soon you will find the Elden boy's grave and another interpretive sign, 35°13.637'N, 111°36.144'W. After the grave site, go SW a short distance on the main trail to a junction. Here you find a sign pointing to the "Pipeline" to your left and to "Fire" on your right, 35°13.621'N, 111°36.152'W. Turn left and walk down to the Pipeline Road, 35°13.554'N, 111°36.129'W. At the road turn left and walk the road back to your car.

Photo: Dick is looking into the little pool formed by the waters of Elden Spring. It's small but of historic and scenic interest.

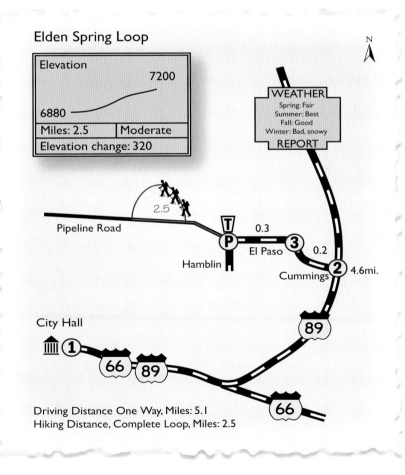

Elden Spring Loop

N

Elevation	
6880	7200
Miles: 2.5	Moderate
Elevation change: 320	

WEATHER
Spring: Fair
Summer: Best
Fall: Good
Winter: Bad, snowy
REPORT

2.5

Pipeline Road

T
P 0.3

El Paso ③ 0.2

Hamblin ② 4.6mi.

Cummings

City Hall

① 89

66 89

66

Driving Distance One Way, Miles: 5.1
Hiking Distance, Complete Loop, Miles: 2.5

Fat Man's Loop Trail #25

Location Map D4
Flagstaff East USGS Map
Flagstaff Trails Map©

Driving One-Way/Total: 5.2/10.4 mi. *8.3/16.6 km* (Time 10/20 minutes)
Access Road: All cars, All paved
Hiking Distance, Complete Loop: 2.4 miles *3.8 km* (Time 2.0 hours)
How Strenuous: Moderate   *Total Drive & Hike Time:* 2 hours 20 min.
Features: Views

NUTSHELL: Located in East Flagstaff at the base of Mt. Elden, this popular trail provides good scenery, variety and views.

DIRECTIONS:
From Flagstaff City Hall (1) Go:
   East, then north on Highway 89. See Access Map, pages 10-11. At 5.2 miles *8.3 km* (MP 419.5) just past the Flagstaff Mall, you will see a trailhead sign and a paved driveway to your left into a parking lot bounded by a pole fence (2). Pull in there and park. 35°13.812'N 111°34.762'W.

TRAILHEAD: At the parking lot.

DESCRIPTION: The Fat Man's Loop and **Elden Lookout Trails** are the same to the 0.2 mile *0.3 km* point. There the Fat Man's branches to the right 35°13.398'N 111°34.913'W. The trail, which up to now has been heading toward Mt. Elden, turns to the north and moves parallel to the base of the mountain.
   At 0.5 miles *0.8 km* is the junction where the **Christmas Tree Trail** goes to your right, 35°14.178'N 111°34.888'W. Soon after you reach a narrow gap between two boulders that gives the Fat Man's Trail its name, since a fat man could not squeeze through it: 35°14.518'N 111°35.000'W.
   At 0.9 miles *1.4 km* you are high enough to get some views and turn to the south. To your right the open plain is Doney Park. To your left you see immense cliffs on Mt. Elden. These are made of columns of lava caused by huge volcanic outbursts two million years ago. All through this area you will see volcanic boulders, some of them big as a house, with interesting shapes.
   You reach the high point of the trail at 1.5 miles *2.4 km*, where there is another trail junction 35°14.367'N 111°35.102'W. The path to the right is the **Elden Lookout Trail**, which is not for fat men as it is a very steep climb. You take the trail to the left, from where it is all downhill back to the starting point. At 1.9 miles *3.0 km* you will pass the junction with the **Pipeline Trail**. 35°14.058'N 111°35.102'W. From here it is 0.5 miles *0.8 km* back to your car.

Photo: This is the narrow gap between boulders that gives the trail its name. The idea is that a fat man could not get through it. Want to test yourself?

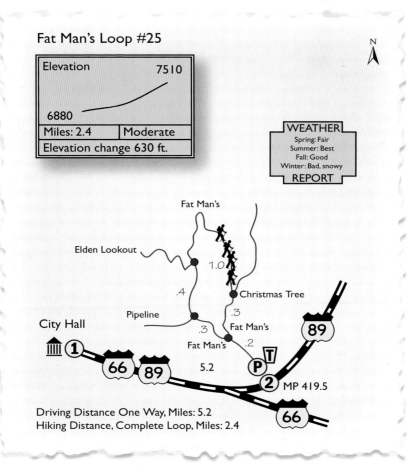

Fat Man's Loop #25

Elevation 7510
6880
Miles: 2.4 | Moderate
Elevation change 630 ft.

WEATHER
Spring: Fair
Summer: Best
Fall: Good
Winter: Bad, snowy
REPORT

Fat Man's

Elden Lookout
1.0

.4
Christmas Tree
.3
Pipeline
.3 Fat Man's
.2
Fat Man's
89

City Hall
1
66 89
5.2
P T
2 MP 419.5
66

Driving Distance One Way, Miles: 5.2
Hiking Distance, Complete Loop, Miles: 2.4

Fay Canyon

Location Map E4
Flagstaff East USGS Map
Flagstaff Trails Map©

Driving One-Way/Total: 6.8/13.6 mi. *10.9/21.8 km* (Time 20/40 minutes)
Access Road: All cars, Last 0.1 miles *0.2 km* good gravel road
Hiking One-Way/Total: 2.6/5.2 mi. *4.2/8.3 km* (Time 1.0/2.0 hours)
How Strenuous: Moderate   *Total Drive & Hike Time:* 2 hours 40 min.
Features: Nice canyon, Easy to reach

NUTSHELL: Fay Canyon is one of a number of limestone-walled canyons that feed into Walnut Canyon south of Flagstaff.

DIRECTIONS:
From Flagstaff City Hall (1) Go:
West, then south on Route 66 under the railroad overpass. At 0.5 miles *0.8 km,* leave Route 66 and go straight on Milton Road. See Access Map, page 10. At 1.7 miles *2.7 km* turn right at the light onto Forest Meadows Street. Go one block to Beulah. Turn left on Beulah and follow it south. Beulah merges onto Highway 89A. At 2.4 miles *3.8 km* (MP 401.6), turn left onto the Lake Mary Road (2). Follow the Lake Mary Road to the 6.7 mile *10.7 km* point (3) where you turn left onto S. Wildlife Drive. Take the first gravel road to the left, which is blocked with a sign closing the road to motor vehicles. Drive up the road just far enough to find a place to pull off and park (there is no assigned parking place), 35°08.043'N, 111°36.933'W.

TRAILHEAD: Walk up the gravel road for 0.4 miles *0.6 km* where you reach the top of a grade and the road goes through a fence. Walk through the fence and immediately take the footpath to the left that you find there, 35°08.111'N, 111°37.345'W.

DESCRIPTION: There is no sign at the fence but you will see one about ten yards down the trail. It advises bikers to be aware of heavy horse traffic.
The trail soon leaves the old road it is following and winds down to the bottom of Fay Canyon, which you reach at 35°08.308'N, 111°37.413'W. From this point the trail is very easy to follow as it runs along Fay Canyon. The canyon is attractive, with walls high enough to be interesting but not overpowering. The trail switches sides from time to time and near the end there is an attractive passage where it climbs high up the north bank.
The trail ends at 35°09.138'N, 111°36.228'W, near Fisher Point. You can walk SE for 0.4 miles *0.6 km* to meet the Arizona Trail at Fisher Point.

Photo: This hike is especially nice in the fall when the leaves are changing color, adding a pleasant note.

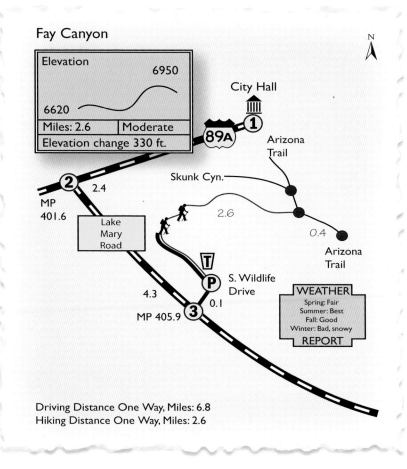

Fay Canyon

N

Elevation

6950

6620

Miles: 2.6	Moderate

Elevation change 330 ft.

City Hall

89A ①

Arizona Trail

② 2.4

MP 401.6

Skunk Cyn.

2.6

0.4

Arizona Trail

Lake Mary Road

T

P   S. Wildlife Drive

4.3

MP 405.9 ③   0.1

WEATHER
Spring: Fair
Summer: Best
Fall: Good
Winter: Bad, snowy
REPORT

Driving Distance One Way, Miles: 6.8
Hiking Distance One Way, Miles: 2.6

Fort Valley Trail

Location Map D3
Humphreys Peak USGS Map
Flagstaff Trails Map©

NEW

Driving One-Way/Total: 4.7/9.4 mi. *7.5/15.0 km* (Time 20/40 minutes)
Access Road: All cars, Last 0.2 miles *0.3 km* paved/then good unpaved
Hiking One-Way/Total: 2.5/5.0 mi. *4.0/8.0 km* (Time 1.5/3.0 hours)
How Strenuous: Moderate   *Total Drive & Hike Time:* 3 hours 40 min.
Features: Trail winds through pine forest from Highway 180 to join the **Schultz Creek Trail**.

NUTSHELL: A meandering walk through the pines north of town

DIRECTIONS:
From Flagstaff City Hall (1) Go:
    North on Humphreys St. for 0.6 miles *1.0 km*. See Access Map, page 10. Turn left at the light onto Hwy 180, the Grand Canyon Road. At 4.5 miles *7.2 km* (MP 220.1) (2) turn right on paved road, then turn right on first gravel road, FR 164B. Go straight onto dirt road, turn left and park at 35°14.980'N 111°41.219'W.

TRAILHEAD: May not be marked, but look for single-track bike path coming out of the forest at the parking spot.

DESCRIPTION: Mountain bikers are heavy users of this trail because it gives them access to a network of trails on the San Francisco Peaks and Mt. Elden/Dry Lake Hills. There are many trails here but when in doubt just take the one most-often used by the bikes.
    The trail moves eastward through an area where there are many finger ridges with shallow valleys in between each ridge. Generally the trail moves around the head of each valley but it does dip down into a few of them. The forest has been thinned here, giving an idea of the advantages of thinning.
    You will come to several trail junctions, marked with post-mounted maps. For GPS users, the junctions are as follows: First Junction, go right: 35°15.248'N 111°40.509'W. Second Junction, go right: 35°15.254'N 111°40.466'W. Third Junction, go straight: 35°15.084'N 111°40.277'W. Fourth Junction (old road), go straight: 35°14.984'N 111°40.022.W. Fifth Junction (Schultz Pass Road), go straight: 35°14.996'N 111°39.989'W. Hike downhill on old road to join the Schultz Creek Trail at 35°15.086'N 111°39.932'W.
    The signs seem to indicate that the trail ends at the Fourth Junction, a funny place to quit. Going on down to the Schultz Creek Trail is better. There are the remains of an old CCC camp in that vicinity. Turn left to see them.

Photo: There is an aggressive program underway to thin the forest around Flagstaff, to restore it to its pristine state. The results are visible here.

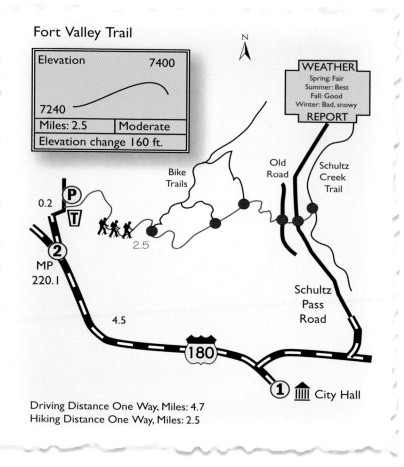

Fort Valley Trail

Elevation	7400
7240	
Miles: 2.5	Moderate
Elevation change 160 ft.	

N

WEATHER
Spring: Fair
Summer: Best
Fall: Good
Winter: Bad, snowy
REPORT

Bike Trails

Old Road

Schultz Creek Trail

0.2

P
T

2.5

2

MP 220.1

Schultz Pass Road

4.5

180

1 City Hall

Driving Distance One Way, Miles: 4.7
Hiking Distance One Way, Miles: 2.5

Grand Falls

Location Map B5
Grand Falls USGS Map
Coconino Forest Service Map

Driving One-Way/Total: 38.8/77.6 mi. *62.1/124.2 km* (Time 1.0/2.0 hours)
Access Road: All cars, Last 9.1 miles *14.6 km* medium gravel road
Hiking One-Way/Total: 0.75/1.5 mi. *1.2/2.4 km* (Time 45/90 minutes)
How Strenuous: Moderate   *Total Drive & Hike Time:* 3.5 hours
Features: Waterfall, Painted Desert Views, Peaks views

NUTSHELL: Located east of Flagstaff, Grand Falls is Arizona's biggest waterfall, with a drop higher than Niagara's. A trail goes down to the water.

DIRECTIONS:
From Flagstaff City Hall (1) Go:
    East, then north on Highway 89. See Access Map, pages 10-11. At 6.5 miles *10.4 km* (MP 420.5) turn right onto the Townsend-Winona Road (2). Follow it to the 14.7 miles *23.5 km* point (MP 428.8) (3) where you turn left on the Leupp Road. At 29.7 miles *47.5 km* (MP 443.5) (4), turn left on Navajo Route 70. At 38.3 miles *61.3 km* turn left (4), 35°25.512'N, 111°11.648'W. You will reach the picnic area at 38.8 miles *62.1 km* where you will see several shelters. Park near the highest shelter, 35°25.667'N, 111°12.005'W.

TRAILHEAD: At the end of the road past the last (lower) picnic shelter, 35°25.694'N, 111°12.258'W.

DESCRIPTION: This is best taken when the Little Colorado River is running high, during spring snow melt in March and April or after a hard rain. From the parking place you will see other shelters downstream. You can drive to the last one, but the road there is really rough. Walk down the road. When you reach the last shelter, you will see that the road continues a short distance to the rim. The end of the road is the trailhead (unmarked).
    The unmaintained unmarked trail goes to the river bottom. Once there you can walk along the shore toward the falls and—depending on how muddy it is—you can get quite close to them. The high dirt content of the water accounts for the color and thickness of the falls, which look like cocoa. It is dangerous to hike behind the falls when water is running.
    The falls spill over a limestone wall, whereas the trailside wall is basalt lava. An eruption from Merriam Crater seven miles to the west poured this lava into the canyon, damming the river and changing its course. A thin finger of lava, still visible, also flowed 15 miles along the riverbed before freezing into rock.

Photo: The trick to this adventure is to visit the falls when there is a heavy flow of water. At such times, as the photo shows, the results are spectacular.

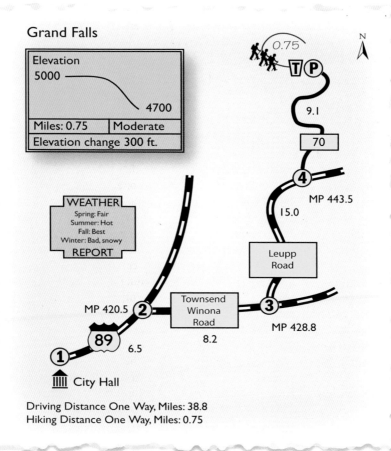

Grand Falls

Elevation	
5000 — 4700	
Miles: 0.75	Moderate
Elevation change 300 ft.	

0.75

T P

N

9.1

70

4

MP 443.5

15.0

WEATHER
Spring: Fair
Summer: Hot
Fall: Best
Winter: Bad, snowy
REPORT

Leupp
Road

Townsend
Winona
Road

MP 420.5 2

3

MP 428.8

89

6.5

8.2

1

City Hall

Driving Distance One Way, Miles: 38.8
Hiking Distance One Way, Miles: 0.75

Griffiths Spring Canyon Trail

Location Map E3
Mountainaire USGS Map
Flagstaff Trails Map©

Driving One-Way/Total: 7.5/15.0 mi. *12.0/24.0 km* (Time 20/40 minutes)
Access Road: All cars, All paved
Hiking Distance, Complete Loop: 1.2 miles *1.9 km* (Time 40 minutes)
How Strenuous: Easy   ***Total Drive & Hike Time:*** 1 hour 20 min.
Features: Easy to reach trailhead, Near town

NUTSHELL: This is a short easy hike located just south of town on the road to Oak Creek Canyon. It is easy to reach, and has parking and a toilet.

DIRECTIONS:
From Flagstaff City Hall (1) Go:
    West on Route 66 one block then left (south) on Route 66 under the railroad overpass. At 0.5 miles *0.8 km*, go straight on Milton Road. See Access Map, page 10. At 1.7 miles *2.7 km* turn right at the light at Forest Meadows. At the next corner turn left on Beulah and follow it out of town. Beulah will connect onto Highway 89A, the road to Oak Creek Canyon. At 7.5 miles *12.0 km* (MP 396.5) (2) turn left into the signed parking area. 35°06.926'N 111°42.616'W.

TRAILHEAD: At the parking area. This is a developed trail.

DESCRIPTION: From the parking lot you walk about 0.2 miles *0.3 km* on a crushed gravel path to a point where you join the loop 35°06.833'N 111°42.476'W. You can go either to the left or to the right here and wind up back at this point. We suggest going to the left. You will walk northward through the forest to the far end of the loop and then curve downhill to the east and begin walking south along the rim of the canyon.
    The canyon is wide and shallow here and there usually is a small stream from the spring flowing in the bottom. As you proceed south, the canyon deepens and becomes more interesting. In order to protect the fragile riparian habitat, the trail does not go into the canyon itself but there are viewpoints where you can look down into it.
    At the south end of the loop you curve away from the canyon and return to the connector that takes you back to the parking lot.
    Griffith Spring itself is located north of the trail, and you will not even see it on this walk.

Photo: This nice little trail looks out onto the grassy floor of a canyon close to town, for an easy but interesting hike.

Griffiths Spring Canyon Trail

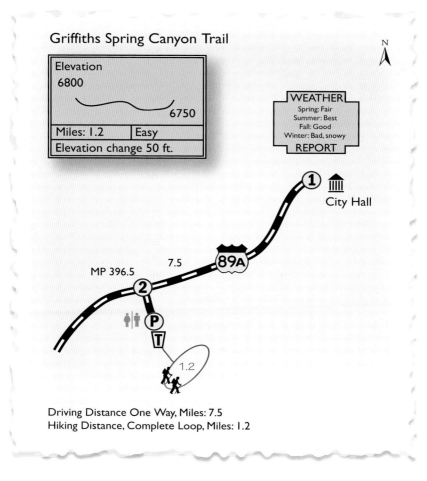

Elevation 6800	
6750	
Miles: 1.2	Easy
Elevation change 50 ft.	

WEATHER
Spring: Fair
Summer: Best
Fall: Good
Winter: Bad, snowy
REPORT

N

(1) 🏛 City Hall

89A

MP 396.5   7.5

(2)

🚻 (P) (T) 1.2

Driving Distance One Way, Miles: 7.5
Hiking Distance, Complete Loop, Miles: 1.2

Heart Trail #103

Location Map D4
Flagstaff East & Sunset Crater West USGS Maps
Flagstaff Trails Map©

Driving One-Way/Total: 7.0/14.0 mi. *11.2/22.4 km* (Time 15/30 minutes)
Access Road: All cars, Last 0.1 mile *0.2 km* good dirt road
Hiking One-Way/Total: 3.8/7.6 mi. *6.1/12.2 km* (Time 2.5/5.0 hours)
How Strenuous: Hard   *Total Drive & Hike Time:* 5½ hours
Features: Unusual red and white hills, Rock formations, Views

NUTSHELL: This trail, located just 7.0 miles *11.2 km* from City Hall, takes you up a red hill on the east face of Mt. Elden.

DIRECTIONS:
From Flagstaff City Hall (1) Go:
    East, then north on Highway 89. See Access Map, pages 10-11. At 6.5 miles *10.4 km* (MP 420.7), you will pass the light at the junction of Highway 89 and the Townsend-Winona Road. Look for a dirt road (FR 9129) going into the trees to your left 0.4 miles *0.6 km* beyond the stoplight, at 6.9 miles *11.0 km* (MP 421.1) (2). Take this dirt road to the parking area at the fence, at 7.0 miles *11.2 km.* 35°15.012'N 111°33.737'W

TRAILHEAD: There are trail signs. You hike the **Sandy Seep Trail** to reach the Heart Trail trailhead.

DESCRIPTION: The trail is an old closed road and is easy to walk. It winds through the forest and at 1.0 miles *1.6 km* comes to a hill. The road curves around it. At 1.4 miles *2.2 km* you arrive at the end of the **Christmas Tree Trail** coming in from your left, 35°15.305'N 111°34.713'W. Turn right and hike to the 1.5 mile *2.4 km* point, where the Sandy Seep Trail ends and the Heart Trail begins, 35°15.398'N 111°34.771'W. Sandy Seep is to your right, a low area.
    You will walk toward Mt. Elden, gaining altitude all the way. The soil here is red. There are two Sedona-like redrock hills to your right and a red foothill projecting from the face of Mt. Elden. At 2.1 miles *3.4 km* you reach the base of the red foothill, where there is a water tank.
    From this point the trail switchbacks up the red hill to the top of Mt. Elden. Sherry, with her photographer's eye, says this part of the trail is *visually exciting.* There are many bold and unusual lava dike formations, totem-like burnt trees, vast views to the east, finger ridges running parallel to the hill you are climbing and other delights. The trail ends atop Mt. Elden where you meet the **Sunset Trail,** 35°15.608'N 111°36.085'W.

Photo: Coming down from the top of Mt. Elden, this steep trail has many open vistas to make the effort of hiking it worthwhile.

Heart Trail #103

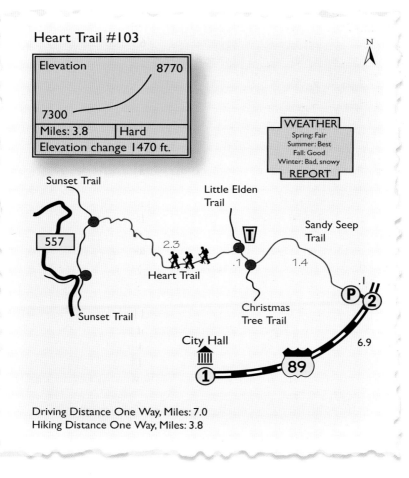

Elevation 8770

7300

Miles: 3.8	Hard
Elevation change 1470 ft.	

WEATHER
Spring: Fair
Summer: Best
Fall: Good
Winter: Bad, snowy
REPORT

Sunset Trail

Little Elden Trail

Sandy Seep Trail

557

2.3

Heart Trail

.1

1.4

Sunset Trail

Christmas Tree Trail

City Hall

89

P

2

.1

6.9

1

Driving Distance One Way, Miles: 7.0
Hiking Distance One Way, Miles: 3.8

Humphreys Trail #151

Location Map C3
Humphreys Peak USGS Map
Coconino Forest Service Map

Driving One-Way/Total: 13.9/27.8 mi. *22.2/44.5 km* (Time 30/60 minutes)
Access Road: All cars, All paved except for parking lot
Hiking One-Way/Total: 4.8/9.6 mi. *7.7/15.4 km* (Time 3.5/7.0 hours)
How Strenuous: Hard   *Total Drive & Hike Time:* 8 hours
Features: Highest point in Arizona, Alpine forests, Unsurpassed views

NUTSHELL: Starting at the Snow Bowl, north of Flagstaff, this strenuous climb takes you to the top of Mt. Humphreys, the highest point in Arizona.

DIRECTIONS:
From Flagstaff City Hall (1) Go:
North on Humphreys Street for 0.6 miles *1.0 km.* See Access Map, page 10. Turn left at the stoplight onto Highway 180. At 7.1 miles *11.4 km* (MP 223) (2), turn right onto Snow Bowl Road. At the top at 13.7 miles *21.9 km* you will see a big sign for the trail. Turn left to the parking area. Drive out to the end of the loop and park near the sign, at 13.9 miles *22.2 km*, 35°19.879'N, 111°42.695'W.

TRAILHEAD: At the parking lot. You will see a sign

DESCRIPTION: Begin by walking across an open meadow to a forest on the other side. The forest in the first couple of miles is a heavy one of fir, spruce and aspen. There are many fallen timbers, making a tangle on the floor. The trees are tall, shutting out most of the sun. It's dark and you have no views.

As you go higher, the forest opens and you will encounter small meadows which permit views to the west. At about the 10,500 foot point the aspens begin to disappear. You can see from here into the Snow Bowl area. What appear to be roads there are actually the ski runs cut through the trees.

The forest thins as you climb until the only trees are twisted and stunted bristlecone pines. There is no cover for the trail here and the footing is not very good. At 3.8 miles *6.1 km* you reach the rim where the Humphreys Trail joins the **Weatherford Trail** coming in from your right, and are above timberline, 35°20.104'N, 111°40.900'W. You can look into the Inner Basin for a splendid view and can also see to the east for the first time.

Above timberline it is bare and almost always windy and cold. The footing is tricky, a mixture of loose gravel and rough jagged lava. You can't really walk along the crest but must walk below it. To get to the top of Mt. Humphreys take the path to the left. The top is 1.0 miles *1.6 km* away, 35°20.778'N, 111°40.678'W.

Photo: The trail makes its way up to the top of Mt. Humphreys, the highest point in Arizona. Below timberline it passes through a heavy mixed forest.

Humphreys Trail #151

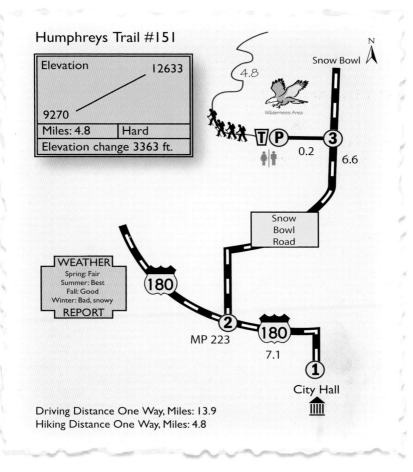

Elevation	12633
9270	
Miles: 4.8	Hard
Elevation change 3363 ft.	

4.8

Snow Bowl

N

Wilderness Area

T P

0.2

3

6.6

Snow Bowl Road

WEATHER
Spring: Fair
Summer: Best
Fall: Good
Winter: Bad, snowy
REPORT

180

2

MP 223

180

7.1

1

City Hall

Driving Distance One Way, Miles: 13.9
Hiking Distance One Way, Miles: 4.8

Inner Basin Trail #29

Location Map C3
Humphreys Peak and Sunset Crater West USGS Maps
Flagstaff Trails Map©

Driving One-Way/Total: 21.6/43.2 mi. *34.6/69.1 km* (Time 45/90 minutes)
Access Road: All cars, Last 4.5 miles *7.2 km* medium dirt road
Hiking One-Way/Total: 3.9/7.8 mi. *6.2/12.5 km* (Time 2.0/4.0 hours)
How Strenuous: Hard   *Total Drive & Hike Time:* 5.5 hours
Features: High mountain, Alpine forests, Great views

NUTSHELL: This is an alpine hike to the beautiful Inner Basin of the San Francisco Peaks.

DIRECTIONS:
From Flagstaff City Hall (1) Go:
    East, then north on Highway 89. See Access Map, pages 10-11. At 17.1 miles *27.4 km* (MP 431.2)—even with the entrance to Sunset Crater (2)—turn left, go across the highway onto unpaved FR 420 and follow the signs to Lockett Meadow, which you will reach at 21.6 miles *34.6 km.*

TRAILHEAD: Drive all the way back through the campsites into the day use area. You'll see a day use parking area with toilet midway. Drive past and park at the trailhead, 35°21.413'N 111°37.387'W. If it is full, then loop back and you will find more parking spaces.

DESCRIPTION: The trail is a road used by the City of Flagstaff for access to the watershed. You will climb constantly through a beautiful alpine forest.
    At 1.6 miles *2.6 km* you come to a point where there are green cabins, 35°20.771'N 111°38.636'W. A faucet there *sometimes* runs with untreated spring water. The **Waterline Trail** (FR 146) crosses through here.
    Go straight ahead. At 2.0 miles *3.2 km* you will break out of the timber into a bare area. This is the Inner Basin. The trail continues through the basin, rising as it goes. As it approaches the rim, it makes a steep climb to the top, ending where it joins the **Weatherford Trail,** at 35°19.625'N, 111°40.041'W, at a great viewpoint.
    The Inner Basin of the Peaks has a tremendous amount of water because snow melting inside the crater gathers in the bowl and as a result there are several springs. Flagstaff realized the importance of the basin as a water supply and sewed up the water rights. As a result most of the Inner Basin's water is captured, sent to the city through underground pipes; so you will see very little of it on the surface. Even so, the Inner Basin is a splendid scenic place.

Photo: This is a hike we take every fall, about mid-October, in order to see the golden leaves of the aspen trees.

Inner Basin Trail #29

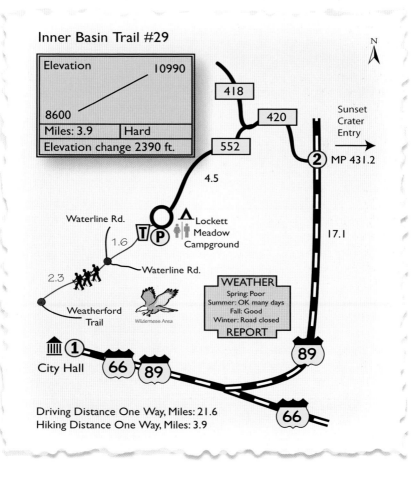

Elevation	10990
8600	
Miles: 3.9	Hard
Elevation change 2390 ft.	

418

420

Sunset
Crater
Entry →

552

② MP 431.2

4.5

Waterline Rd.

T P ♿ Lockett
Meadow
Campground

17.1

1.6

2.3

Waterline Rd.

Weatherford
Trail

Wilderness Area

WEATHER
Spring: Poor
Summer: OK many days
Fall: Good
Winter: Road closed
REPORT

🏛 ①

City Hall 66 89

89

66

Driving Distance One Way, Miles: 21.6
Hiking Distance One Way, Miles: 3.9

Kachina Trail #150

Location Map C3
Humphreys Peak USGS Map
Flagstaff Trails Map©

Driving One-Way/Total: 13.9/27.8 mi. *22.2/44.5 km* (Time 30/60 minutes)
Access Road: All cars, paved except for last bit to trailhead
Hiking One-Way/Total: 4.9/9.8 mi. *7.8/15.7 km* (Time 2.5/5.0 hours)
How Strenuous: Hard   ***Total Drive & Hike Time:*** 6 hours
Features: High mountains, Alpine forests, Excellent views

NUTSHELL: This hike across the south face of the San Francisco Peaks displays the mountain forests at their best. **A personal favorite.**

DIRECTIONS:
From Flagstaff City Hall (1) Go:
   North on Humphreys Street for 0.6 miles *1.0 km*. See Access Map, page 10. Turn left at the light onto Highway 180, the Grand Canyon road. At 7.1 miles *11.4 km* (MP 223) (2), turn right on the Snow Bowl Road. Drive up the Snow Bowl Road to the 13.7 miles *21.9 km* point where you see a sign for the Kachina Trail. Turn right and drive 0.2 miles *0.3 km,* parking near the trailhead.

TRAILHEAD: Just beyond the parking lot. 35°19.595'N 111°42.693'W.

DESCRIPTION: This trail starts at 9,360 feet and winds easterly across the south face (Flagstaff side) of the Peaks. Most of the hike holds to a contour between the 9,200 and 8,800 foot levels, rising and falling within this band. The trail passes through a lovely forest of fir, spruce and aspen. This is a good trail to take in the fall to see the changing aspen leaves.
   You will pass interesting lava boulders and cliffs. In places you will find clearings that give you views out over the countryside. At one point you will enter Freidlein Prairie, a beautiful park, visible from Flagstaff. You will walk near the foot of the prairie, enjoying breathtaking views up the mountain, with Fremont and Doyle Peaks on the skyline.
   The trail ends in an open area where it meets an old road, 35°17.950'N 111°38.905'W. This is the historic Weatherford Road. This is the official way the trail is laid out, making for a hard uphill return.
   We like to take two cars, parking the "catcher car" at the lower end (see map). After you have gone up the Snow Bowl Rd. 2.4 miles *3.8 km*, turn onto the Freidlein Prairie Road FR 522 and drive both cars to the secondary parking area, 35°17.822'N 111°39.086'W. Park one car and take the other to the upper trailhead. Done this way, the entire hike is 5.3 miles *8.5 km* long.

Photo: This photo shows why the Kachina Trail is one of our favorites, as the scenery is varied and magnificent.

Kachina Trail #150

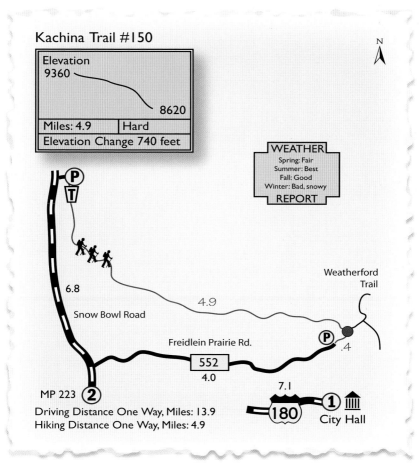

Elevation
9360
8620

Miles: 4.9 | Hard
Elevation Change 740 feet

N

WEATHER
Spring: Fair
Summer: Best
Fall: Good
Winter: Bad, snowy
REPORT

Weatherford
Trail

6.8

4.9

Snow Bowl Road

Freidlein Prairie Rd.

552
4.0

.4

P

P
T

MP 223 (2)

7.1

180 (1) City Hall

Driving Distance One Way, Miles: 13.9
Hiking Distance One Way, Miles: 4.9

Kelsey Spring-Winter Cabin Trail

Location Map F2
Sycamore Point USGS Map
Coconino Forest Service Map

Driving One-Way/Total: 26.3/52.6 mi. *42.1/84.2 km* (Time 1.0/2.0 hours)
Access Road: High clearance needed for last 0.6 miles *1.0 km*
Hiking One-Way/Total: 7.55/15.1 mi. *12.1/24.2 km* (Time 4.0/8.0 hours)
How Strenuous: Hard   *Total Drive & Hike Time:* 10 hours
Features: Springs, Pristine forests, Views

NUTSHELL: Scenic trail moving along the side of Sycamore Canyon.

DIRECTIONS:
From Flagstaff City Hall (1) Go:
    West, then south on Route 66 beneath the railroad overpass. See Access Map, page 10. At 0.5 miles *0.8 km* turn right on Route 66. At 2.6 miles *4.2 km* turn left on Woody Mountain Road, FR 231 (2). It is partly paved. At 16.6 miles *26.6 km* turn right onto FR 538 (3) and follow it to the 22.3 mile *35.7 km* point, a T junction (4). Turn left on FR 538, and drive to the 25.7 mile *41.1 km* point (5). Turn right on FR 538H, a rough road, and go to its end at 26.3 miles *42.1 km*. Park at the end of the road, 35°01.366'N, 111°55.488'W.

TRAILHEAD: At the sign at the parking area.

DESCRIPTION: You first hike 1.25 miles *2.0 km* to **Winter Cabin.** From the cabin walk a few steps down the trail and you will find a marker for the Kelsey-Winter Trail. You turn to the right and go downhill, crossing a ravine until you reach the 6200 foot level.
    From this point the trail moves along the side of the canyon, pretty much on the 6200 foot contour. The first part of the trail is wooded but you will break out into the clear, which allows you to enjoy views of Sycamore Canyon, a spectacular sight. This trail is little used and there are rough patches where it moves through scratchy shrubs.
    You reach **Dorsey Spring** at 3.85 miles *6.2 km*. The trail turns right uphill to the actual spring, which is at 35°03.255'N, 111°56.736'W. Water usually flows from the spring but it can run dry, so don't count on it.
    From Dorsey Spring the trail continues to move laterally along the side of the canyon, and is mostly wooded so that canyon views are restricted. You reach a junction, at 6.75 miles *10.8 km*, 35°04.421'N, 111°56.434'W. The Little LO Trail goes to the left. Turn right here and make an uphill climb. You reach Babe's Hole at 6.85 miles *11.0 km,* 35°04.369'N, 111°56.381'W. Keep climbing to the end of the trail at 7.55 miles *15.1 km*, at Kelsey Spring, 35°04.517'N, 111°56.122'W.

Photo: The trees hide the fact that the majestic Sycamore Canyon is just a stone's throw away. In fact, you walk along the side of the canyon.

Kelsey Spring-Winter Cabin Trail

N

Elevation	
6900	
	6320
5900	
5900	

Miles: 7.55	Hard
Elevation change 1000 ft.	

WEATHER
Spring: Fair
Summer: Best
Fall: Good
Winter: Bad, snowy
REPORT

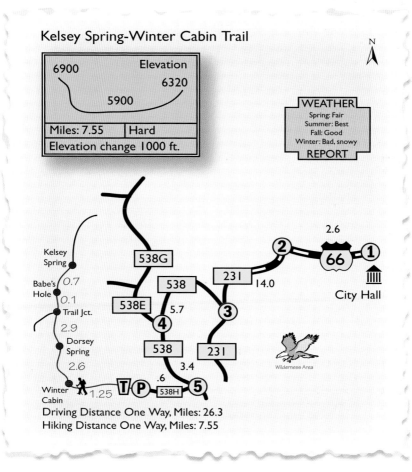

Kelsey Spring

Babe's Hole 0.7

0.1

Trail Jct.

2.9

Dorsey Spring

2.6

Winter Cabin   1.25

538G

538

538E

538

5.7

4

538

3.4

538H   .6

5

231

3

231

14.0

2

66

2.6

1

City Hall

Wilderness Area

T P

Driving Distance One Way, Miles: 26.3
Hiking Distance One Way, Miles: 7.55

Kendrick Trail #22

Location Map C2
Kendrick Peak and Wing Mt. USGS Maps
Kaibab Forest Service Map

Driving One-Way/Total: 20.7/41.4 mi. *33.1/66.2 km* (Time 45/90 minutes)
Access Road: All cars, Last 6.6 miles *10.6 km* good gravel road
Hiking One-Way/Total: 4.6/9.2 mi. *7.4/14.7 km* (Time 2.5/5.0 hours)
How Strenuous: Hard   *Total Drive & Hike Time:* 6.5 hours
Features: Ten thousand foot peak, Views

NUTSHELL: 10,418-foot-tall Kendrick Peak is the eighth-tallest peak in Arizona. This trail winds to its summit for great views.

DIRECTIONS:
From Flagstaff City Hall (1) Go:
   North on Humphreys Street for 0.6 miles *1.0 km*. See Access Map, page 10. Turn left at the light onto Highway 180, the Grand Canyon Road. At 14.1 miles *22.6 km* (MP 230.1) (2) turn left on FR 245, and follow it to the 17.1 mile *27.4 km* point (3). Turn right on FR 171 and follow it to the 20.2 mile *32.3 km* point, where you will see a sign for the trail (4). Turn right on FR 190, and drive into the parking lot at 20.7 miles *33.1 km*. There is a toilet at the lot.

TRAILHEAD: At the parking area, 35°23.207'N, 111°52.052'W.

DESCRIPTION: A forest fire in 2000 caused extensive damage to Kendrick Mountain. See details on the trailhead sign. The fire damage is evident.
   You will walk along a footpath to the 0.7 mile *1.1 km* point, where you join an old road, now closed. From here the trail follows an unending series of steep switchbacks.
   At 2.0 miles *3.2 km* the road ends and you follow a footpath. This is a good path, following the contours of the mountain intelligently and providing good footing. It was built as a working trail so that rangers could reach the fire lookout tower by horseback.
   From a distance you will notice that Kendrick Peak has one definite sharp point, not a series of peaks like its neighbor, the San Francisco Peaks. You will reach a flat area just below the absolute peak at about 4.1 miles *6.6 km*. 35°24.476'N 111°51.009'W. Here you will find the Old Ranger Cabin. It was built in the years 1911-1912 and was saved from the 2000 fire. The **Bull Basin Trail** terminates just behind the cabin. The **Pumpkin Trail** ends on the other side of the clearing.
   From this flat there is one last climb to the tower, reached at 4.6 miles *7.4 km*.

Photo: Kendrick is one of the highest mountains in Arizona. Even though there are many other peaks in the area, its distinctive peaked tip identifies it.

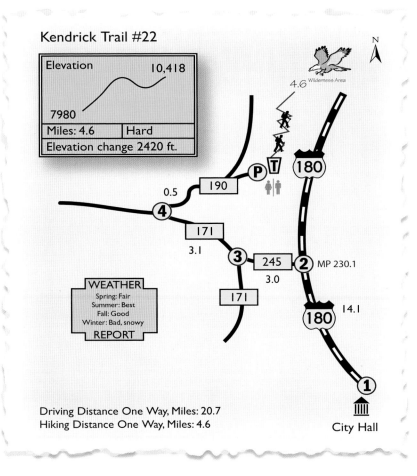

Kendrick Trail #22

Elevation	10,418
7980	
Miles: 4.6	Hard
Elevation change 2420 ft.	

N

4.6 Wilderness Area

0.5   190   P   T

180

4   171

3.1   3   245   2   MP 230.1

3.0

WEATHER
Spring: Fair
Summer: Best
Fall: Good
Winter: Bad, snowy
REPORT

171

180   14.1

1

City Hall

Driving Distance One Way, Miles: 20.7
Hiking Distance One Way, Miles: 4.6

Keyhole Sink #114

Location Map D1
Sitgreaves Mtn. USGS Map
Kaibab Forest Service Map

Driving One-Way/Total: 22.4/44.8 mi. *35.8/71.7 km* (Time 40/80 minutes)
Access Road: All cars, All paved
Hiking One-Way/Total: 0.75/1.5 mi. *1.2/2.4 km* (Time 25/50 minutes)
How Strenuous: Easy   *Total Drive & Hike Time:* 2 hours 10 min.
Features: Hidden pond, Cliffs with Indian rock art

NUTSHELL: This easy hike is located in the Parks area, 22.4 miles *35.8 km* west of Flagstaff. It follows a little canyon into a picturesque rounded box. Water is dammed there by cliffs on which are scratched Indian rock art.

DIRECTIONS:
From Flagstaff City Hall (1) Go:
    West a block on Route 66, then south, beneath the railroad overpass. See the Access Map on page 10. At 0.5 miles *0.8 km* take the right fork, staying on Route 66. You soon leave town. At 5.0 miles *8.0 km* you merge onto I-40 West. Drive I-40W, to the 18.0 mile *28.8 km* point, where you take Exit 178, Parks Road (2). Turn right at the stop sign and go to the 18.4 mile *29.4 km* point, where there is a second stop sign. Turn left (3). You are now on old Route 66 heading west. At the 19.0 mile *30.4 km* point you pass the Parks Store (right). Keep going west to the 22.4 mile *35.8 km* point (4), then turn left into the Oak Hill Snow Play Area parking lot 35°15.701'N 112°00.651'W.

TRAILHEAD: Walk north, across Route 66, to the green gate.

DESCRIPTION: The trail follows a small canyon that curves down into a deeper canyon, where you will see a thick grove of spindly aspens, many of them dead.
    You walk a short distance along the canyon bottom to a fence made of aspen logs. An interpretive sign is located at the gate, along with a Guest Register 35°16.107'N 112°00.956'W. Sign in and then go through the fence into a charming little bowl where the canyon ends against high lava cliffs.
    Walk toward the farthest, blackest cliff. There is usually a water pond at its base. As you face the cliff, look for rock art on the cliff faces to the left of the blackest face. There are two major panels of rock art with a few more figures scattered here and there. The panel shown on the interpretive sign is to your left as you face the end cliff.
    This is a natural waterhole for game. It would also be a trap for any animal cornered against the cliffs.

Photo: The lava cliffs catch water in a box canyon. In addition to being a water source, the box worked as a game trap for ancient hunters.

Keyhole Sink #114

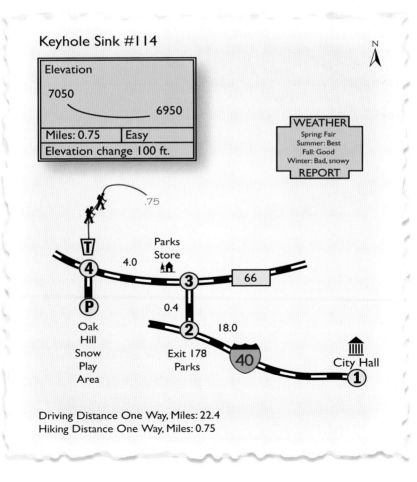

Elevation	
7050 6950	
Miles: 0.75	Easy
Elevation change 100 ft.	

WEATHER
Spring: Fair
Summer: Best
Fall: Good
Winter: Bad, snowy
REPORT

N

.75

Parks Store

4.0

66

0.4

18.0

Oak
Hill
Snow
Play
Area

Exit 178
Parks

40

City Hall

Driving Distance One Way, Miles: 22.4
Hiking Distance One Way, Miles: 0.75

Lakeview Trail #132

Location Map F5
Mormon Lake & Mormon Mtn. USGS Maps
Coconino Forest Service Map

Driving One-Way/Total: 28.0/56.0 mi. *44.8/89.6 km* (Time 35/70 minutes)
Access Road: All cars, All paved
Hiking One-Way/Total: 1.35/2.7 mi. *2.2/4.3 km* (Time 40/80 minutes)
How Strenuous: Moderate **Total Drive & Hike Time:** 2 hours 30 min.
Features: Beautiful forest, Excellent views

NUTSHELL: This hike climbs a ridge on Mormon Mtn. to a viewpoint.

DIRECTIONS:
From Flagstaff City Hall (1) Go:
    West, then south on Route 66 under the railroad overpass. At 0.5 miles *0.8 km*, get onto Milton Road. See Access Map, page 10. At 1.7 miles *2.7 km* turn right onto Forest Meadows and go one block to Beulah. Turn left on Beulah and follow it south. Beulah merges onto Highway 89A. At 2.4 miles *3.8 km* (MP 401.6), turn left onto the Lake Mary Road (2). Follow the Lake Mary Road to the 23.0 mile *36.8 km* point (MP 323.6), where you turn right onto the Mormon Lake Road (3). At 28 miles *44.8 km*, on the Mormon Lake Road, turn right into the Double Springs Campground (4). Park outside the gate at 34°56.552'N 111°29.477'W. If you park inside you must pay a user fee. Walk the road 0.1 mile *0.2 km* to the trailhead. 34°56.531'N 111°29.599'W.

TRAILHEAD: Sign to your left.

DESCRIPTION: At the beginning of the trail you will encounter a little stream. Walk across the two footbridges that span it. The trail goes uphill by the green shack. In 0.1 miles *0.2 km* you will see the official trailhead sign for the Lakeview Trail. It climbs throughout its length but the grade is rather gentle. The Lakeview Trail has been incorporated into the Arizona Trail, which branches off from it at the bottom and the top.
    The forest around Mormon Mountain is beautiful. In addition to Ponderosa pine, there is much oak and some aspen, also many flowers and shrubs.
    For nine-tenths of the hike, the forest through which you pass is dense and you cannot see out. You will wonder why the trail has been given the name Lakeview. Then, as you break out on the top, you can see why. The trail has been climbing gradually up a ridge. As you come to the top of the ridge, you find that its top is a bare lava cliff. The trail ends there at Lakeview Vista 34°55.729'N 111°30.306'W. You can walk back and forth along this area enjoying the views.

Photo: The fact that the end of the trail is a viewpoint is shown here. The lake that it views, Mormon Lake, is sometimes dry, but when full is beautiful.

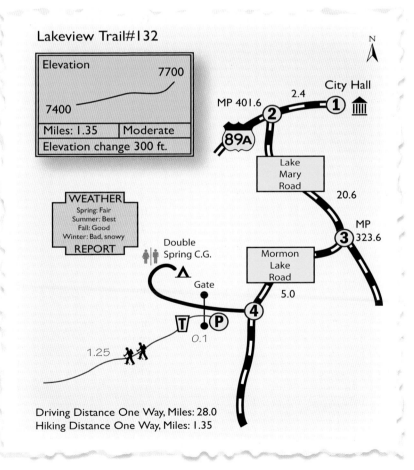

Lakeview Trail#132

N

Elevation	
7400	7700
Miles: 1.35	Moderate
Elevation change 300 ft.	

MP 401.6   2.4   City Hall ①

②

89A

Lake Mary Road

20.6

MP ③ 323.6

WEATHER
Spring: Fair
Summer: Best
Fall: Good
Winter: Bad, snowy
REPORT

Mormon Lake Road

Double Spring C.G.

Gate

5.0

④

T 🚻 P

0.1

1.25

Driving Distance One Way, Miles: 28.0
Hiking Distance One Way, Miles: 1.35

Lava Flow Trail

Location Map C4
Wupatki SW USGS Map
Coconino Forest Service Map

Driving One-Way/Total: 22.1/44.2 mi. *35.4/70.7 km* (Time 30/60 minutes)
Access Road: All cars, All paved
Hiking Distance, Complete Loop: 1.0 mile *1.6 km* (Time 45 minutes)
How Strenuous: Easy   *Total Drive & Hike Time:* 1 hour 45 min.
Features: Views, Extinct volcanoes, Self-guided nature trail

NUTSHELL: This is an easy trail located in the Sunset Crater National Monument 22.1 miles *35.4 km* northeast of Flagstaff. It takes you on a fascinating self-guided nature walk through a volcanic field.

DIRECTIONS:
From Flagstaff City Hall (1) Go:
    East, then north on Highway 89. See Access Map, pages 10-11. At 16.4 miles *26.2 km* (MP 430.3) you will reach the entrance to Sunset Crater National Monument (2). Turn right on the road into Sunset Crater. This road is also known as FR 545. At 18.4 miles *29.4 km* stop at the ticket booth and pay admission. Just beyond is the Visitor Center, worth a look. At 21.9 miles *35.0 km* turn right on road marked Lava Flow Trail Drive (3), and take it to the parking area at 22.1 miles *35.4 km*. 35°21.794'N 111°31.091'W

TRAILHEAD: You will see a sign at the parking area.

DESCRIPTION: This trail is a self-guided walk with points of interest keyed to a guide booklet that is available from a dispenser at the beginning of the trail.
    The trail is paved for a short distance. In fact the Park Service has created a paved short version of the trail for wheelchair use—a nice gesture. On the main trail, once the paving ends, the trail surface is composed of black cinders. A hiker could hurry around the trail in thirty minutes but take your time. Use the booklet and read it at the stopping points.
    Until 1973 visitors could hike to the top of Sunset Crater. Because of the severe erosion that the multitudes of hikers were causing to the face of the crater, hiking on Sunset Crater is now forbidden. The sides of the crater are covered with deep loose black cinders and are therefore unstable. They kept sloughing away from the trails. It is too bad people can't enjoy the experience anymore as we did when we were kids, but the closure was necessary.
    One of the features of this trail is an ice cave, a lava tube such as you encounter on the **Lava River Cave** hike. It was closed in 1992, as it was collapsing.

Photo: If your are interested in volcanoes, then this is the trail for you. You can see red and black lava and immense fields of black cinders.

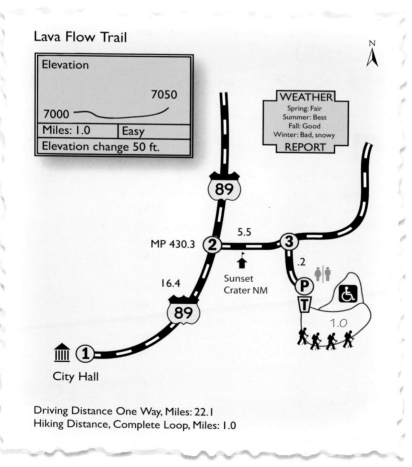

Lava Flow Trail

N

Elevation

7050

7000

Miles: 1.0	Easy
Elevation change 50 ft.	

WEATHER
Spring: Fair
Summer: Best
Fall: Good
Winter: Bad, snowy
REPORT

89

5.5

MP 430.3 2 ─ 3

.2

16.4

Sunset
Crater NM

P

89 T

1.0

🏛 1

City Hall

Driving Distance One Way, Miles: 22.1
Hiking Distance, Complete Loop, Miles: 1.0

Lava River Cave

Location Map C2
Wing Mountain USGS Map
Coconino Forest Service Map

Driving One-Way/Total: 18.45/36.9 mi. *29.5/59.0 km* (Time 40/80 minutes)
Access Road: All cars, Last 4.35 miles *7.0 km* good gravel road
Hiking One-Way/Total: 0.75/1.5 mi. *1.2/2.4 km* (Time 40/80 minutes)
How Strenuous: Moderate   *Total Drive & Hike Time:* 2 hours 40 min.
Features: Unusual underground lava tube

NUTSHELL: This underground lava tube located northwest of Flagstaff is a unique experience.

DIRECTIONS:
From Flagstaff City Hall (1) Go:
    North on Humphreys Street for 0.6 miles *1.0 km*. See Access Map, page 10. Turn left at the light onto Highway 180, the Grand Canyon Road. At 14.1 miles *22.6 km* (MP 230.1) (2), turn left on FR 245, and follow it to the 17.1 mile *27.4 km* point where it meets FR 171 (3). Turn left onto FR 171 and drive it to the 18.2 mile *29.1 km* point, where it intersects FR 171B (4). Turn left on 171B and take it to the 18.45 mile *29.5 km* point where you will find parking, 35°20.562'N, 111°50.267'W.

TRAILHEAD: You will see the trail at the parking area. Walk it to the opening of the cave, which looks like a circular rock wall, 35°20.557'N, 111°50.283'W.

DESCRIPTION: Lava tubes are formed when the outer portion of a river of lava cools while the interior is still hot and flowing. The outer skin forms a hard shell while the inner core flows ahead like water through a straw, leaving an empty tube. This tube was discovered in 1915 by lumberjacks.
    The Forest Service has made a stairway down into the tube using native stone. You have to duck to get into the opening and crawl over fallen stone, but then the tube deepens and you can stand upright. The tube is about 0.75 mile *1.2 km* long. It is chilly, being 32-40°F year-around, coldest near the entrance.
    You must come properly prepared for this hike. A short way past the daylight coming in from the entrance you are in absolute darkness. The floor, ceiling and walls are all extremely rough and uneven and you have to watch every step. Each member of your party should dress warmly, carry a light and have good hiking shoes. We think each person needs two good flashlights with fresh batteries. About halfway you enter a 30 foot-high vault with a side tunnel going off to the right. At the end, the tube pinches closed, like the crimp on the end of a toothpaste tube.

Photo: This somewhat cramped entrance leads to a unique underground hiking experience.

Lava River Cave

N

Elevation	
7680 ⟍⟍⟍ 7580	
Miles: 0.75	Moderate
Elevation change 100 ft.	

WEATHER
The cave is not affected by weather, but the access roads are closed in winter
REPORT

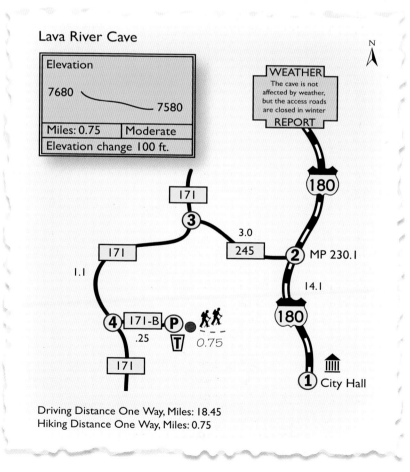

171

③

3.0

171

1.1

245

180

② MP 230.1

14.1

④ 171-B Ⓟ ●

.25 Ⓣ 0.75

171

180

① 🏛 City Hall

Driving Distance One Way, Miles: 18.45
Hiking Distance One Way, Miles: 0.75

Little Bear Trail #112

Location Map D4
Sunset Crater West USGS Map
Flagstaff Trails Map©

Driving One-Way/Total: 11.7/23.4 mi. *18.7/37.4 km* (Time 30/60 minutes)
Access Road: All cars, Last 2.5 miles *4.0 km* fair dirt/gravel road
Hiking One-Way/Total: 4.3/8.6 mi. *6.9/13.8 km* (Time 2.5/5.0 hours)
How Strenuous: Hard   *Total Drive & Hike Time:* 6 hours
Features: Alpine forests, Views

NUTSHELL: This trail, part of the Dry Lake Hills/Mt. Elden system, takes you up to a saddle between the Dry Lake Hills and Little Elden. Along the way you will enjoy tremendous views. **A personal favorite.**

DIRECTIONS:
From Flagstaff City Hall (1) Go:
 East, then north on Highway 89. See Access Map, pages 10-11. At 9.2 miles *14.7 km* (MP 423.3) turn left on a gravel road, FR 556, the Elden Spring Road (2). At 11.7 miles *18.7*, turn right where you see a parking area and pole fence. Park there, 35°16.131'N, 111°36.420'W.

TRAILHEAD: Go through the fence where there is a trail marker, then turn left, toward the road, which you will cross.

DESCRIPTION: You will start this hike by walking a short (0.3 mile *0.5 km*) segment of the Horsecamp Trail, to the point where it joins the **Little Elden Trail**, 35°16.700'N, 111°35.332'W. Then you turn right and walk the Little Elden Trail for 0.6 miles *1.0 km* to reach the Little Bear Trailhead, 35°16.802'N, 111°35.937'W. The length of the Little Bear Trail is 3.4 miles *5.4 km* but you must hike 0.9 miles *1.4 km* to get to it.
 The trail is designed so that it climbs gently, making wide swings as it goes up the grade. You are mostly in heavy tree cover which restricts your views, but you will find a few places where you can make a short detour out to a bare knob and enjoy superb views.
 Throughout the trail you will be hiking on one of the colder spots on the mountain, as a result of which the forest is composed of more firs than pines. In places there are pockets of aspens. This is a pretty place in the fall when the leaves are changing color.
 The trail ends at a saddle where you intersect the **Sunset Trail** 35°16.131'N 111°36.420'W. This makes it possible to connect onto other trails in the Mt. Elden system (see map).

Photo: Taken at the bottom of the trail, about the only level place on it. We like its variety and the fact that it is the only trail off the north face of Mt. Elden.

Little Bear Trail #112

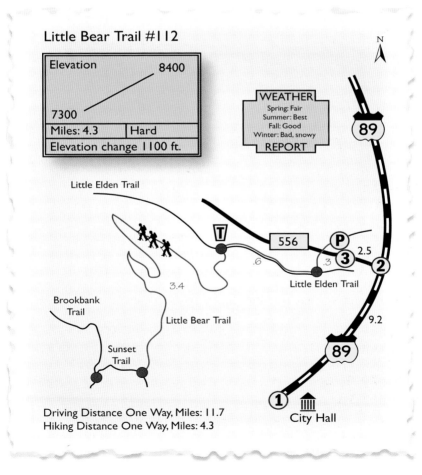

Elevation	8400
7300	
Miles: 4.3	Hard
Elevation change 1100 ft.	

WEATHER
Spring: Fair
Summer: Best
Fall: Good
Winter: Bad, snowy
REPORT

Little Elden Trail

556

Little Elden Trail

Brookbank Trail

Little Bear Trail

Sunset Trail

City Hall

Driving Distance One Way, Miles: 11.7
Hiking Distance One Way, Miles: 4.3

Little Elden Trail #69

Location Map D4
Sunset Crater West USGS Map
Flagstaff Trails Map©

Driving One-Way/Total: 8.7/17.4 mi. *13.9/27.8 km* (Time 30/60 minutes)
Access Road: All cars, Last 5.1 miles *8.2 km* good gravel road
Hiking One-Way/Total: 4.9/9.8 mi. *7.8/15.7 km* (Time 2.5/5.0 hours)
How Strenuous: Moderate   **Total Drive & Hike Time:** 6.0 hours
Features: Beautiful spring, Cliffs, Views

NUTSHELL: Starting at Schultz Tank north of Flagstaff, this trail takes you south around the base of Little Elden Mountain.

DIRECTIONS:
From Flagstaff City Hall (1) Go:
   North on Humphreys Street for 0.6 miles *1.0 km*. See Access Map, page 10. Turn left at the light onto Highway 180, the Grand Canyon Road. At 3.1 miles *5.0 km* (MP 218.6), turn right on the Schultz Pass Road (2). Stay on it to the 8.7 mile *13.9 km* point, where you turn right at the sign for the Weatherford Trail (3). Park in the lot, 35°17.178'N, 111°37.633'W.

TRAILHEAD: At the parking area. Look for the sign.

DESCRIPTION: You walk around the east end of Schultz Tank, to reach a junction with a connector to the **Sunset Trail**, at 35°17.145'N, 111°37.498'W. Go to the left. The trail starts dropping down to the road level, and runs along very close to it.
   At 1.8 miles *2.9 km* you will meet the **Little Bear Trail** as it comes down from the Dry Lake Hills, at 35°16.802'N, 111°35.937'W.
   At 2.4 miles *3.8 km* you reach a junction where a connector to the Horsecamp goes off to the left, 35°16.700'N, 111°35.332'W.
   At 2.6 miles *4.2 km* you reach the entry to Little Elden Spring, where a short trail to the right takes you to the spring.
   Soon after this you round the toe of Little Elden Mountain and curve to the south, entering a bowl formed by the flanks of Little Elden and Mount Elden, a nice remote-feeling place. We like the views of the rocks and cliffs of the mountain in this area. At 4.8 miles *7.7 km* the **Heart Trail** comes down from your right. You walk to the 4.9 mile spot *7.8 km* where the trail ends at its junction with the **Christmas Tree** and **Sandy Seep** trails, 35°15.305'N, 111°34.713'W.

Photo: Dick is looking at the water from Little Elden Spring, one of the features that adds variety to the trail.

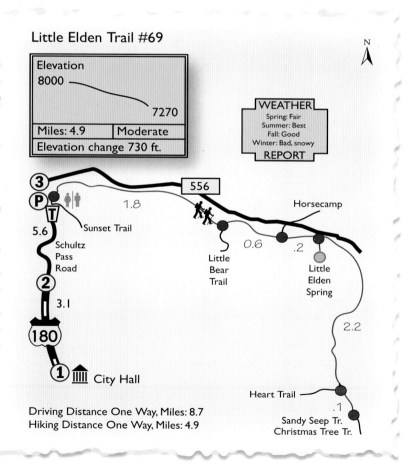

Little Elden Trail #69

N

Elevation 8000 ——— 7270	
Miles: 4.9	Moderate
Elevation change 730 ft.	

WEATHER
Spring: Fair
Summer: Best
Fall: Good
Winter: Bad, snowy
REPORT

③
Ⓟ
Ⓣ
556

5.6   Sunset Trail   1.8   Horsecamp

Schultz
Pass   Little   0.6   .2
Road   Bear
            Trail   Little
②   Elden
                         Spring

3.1

⓵⓼⓪   2.2

①🏛 City Hall

Heart Trail

Driving Distance One Way, Miles: 8.7   .1
Hiking Distance One Way, Miles: 4.9   Sandy Seep Tr.
                                           Christmas Tree Tr.

Little Spring to Bismarck Lake

Location Map C3
Humphreys Peak and White Horse Hills USGS Maps
Coconino Forest Service Map

Driving One-Way/Total: 23.2/46.4 mi. *37.1/74.2 km* (Time 40/80 minutes)
Access Road: High clearance suggested for final 0.2 mi. *0.3 km*
Hiking One-Way/Total: 1.5/3.0 mi. *2.4/4.8 km* (Time 1.0/2.0 hours)
How Strenuous: Moderate   *Total Drive & Hike Time:* 3 hours 20 min.
Features: Beautiful alpine forest, Meadow with lake, Peak views

NUTSHELL: A steep climb through lovely alpine forests to a small lake.

DIRECTIONS:
From Flagstaff City Hall(1) Go:
North on Humphreys Street for 0.6 miles *1.0 km*. See Access Map, page 10. Turn left at the light onto Highway 180, the Grand Canyon Road. Drive to the 19.0 miles *30.4 km* point (MP 235.1)(2), and then turn right on the upper Hart Prairie Road, FR 151. Follow it to the 20.6 miles *33.0 km* point, the junction with FR 418 (3). Turn right on FR 151. At 23.0 miles *36.8 km* turn left on unpaved road and drive to the 23.2 miles *37.1 km* spot, where you park, 35°22.554'N 111°43.991'W.

TRAILHEAD: Hike the old road 0.4 miles *0.6 km* to the spring 35°22.475'N 111°43.534'W which is marked by the greenery that thrives on its water.

DESCRIPTION: Little Spring played an important role in Flagstaff's early days, as it was a stop on the famous Flagstaff-Grand Canyon Stage Coach line. The clearing is a beautiful place to bring the family for a picnic. The spring has been captured and pours through a metal pipe into a small pool.

On the uphill side of the spring you will see a barricade. Hike up the road blocked by the barricade. You will walk up through a beautiful forest of aspen and spruce. This north slope of the mountain seems to get plenty of water. The forest floor is covered with ferns, and on a hike in August we saw mushrooms everywhere.

The first 0.35 miles *0.6 km* of the trail is a bit of a struggle because it is so steep. At this point you will come across an old road. Go to the right (south) here. Soon you will enter a more level area where there is a narrow open park leading toward a large park. From the 0.5 mile *0.8 km* point you will be in sight of the San Francisco Peaks, which look enormous from here.

The trail ends at Bismarck Lake 35°21.902'N 111°43.280'W. Calling this small pond a lake seems like a misnomer, but remember, this is dry Arizona.

Photo: The fence is located behind the spring. Dick is coming down the trail, from Bismarck Lake.

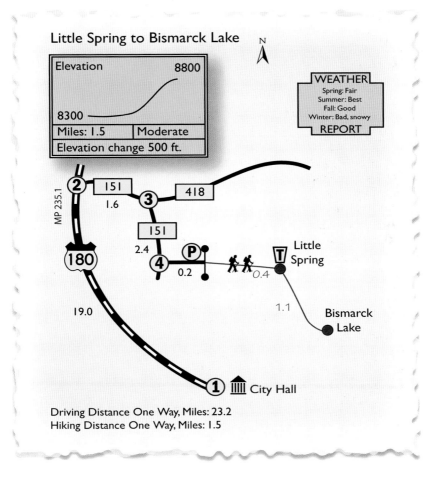

Little Spring to Bismarck Lake

N

Elevation		8800
8300		
Miles: 1.5	Moderate	
Elevation change 500 ft.		

WEATHER
Spring: Fair
Summer: Best
Fall: Good
Winter: Bad, snowy
REPORT

MP 235.1

2 — 151 — 3 — 418
1.6

151
2.4

180

4
0.2

P

Little Spring
T

0.4

19.0

1.1

Bismarck Lake

1 🏛 City Hall

Driving Distance One Way, Miles: 23.2
Hiking Distance One Way, Miles: 1.5

Lookout Trail

Location Map C3
Humphreys Peak USGS Map
Coconino Forest Service Map

Driving One-Way/Total: 14.2/28.4 mi. *22.7/45.4 km* (Time 45/90 minutes)
Access Road: All cars, All paved
Hiking One-Way/Total: 0.4/0.8 mi. *0.6/1.3 km* (30/60 min) Add 1 hour ride
How Strenuous: Moderate   *Total Drive, Ride & Hike Time:* 3.5 hours
Features: High mountains, Alpine forests, Wonderful views

NUTSHELL: You drive to the Snow Bowl and take the Sky Ride. This trail is at the end of the ride.

DIRECTIONS:
From Flagstaff City Hall (1) Go:
    North on Humphreys Street for 0.6 miles *1.0 km.* See Access Map, page 10. Turn left at the light onto Highway 180, the road to the Grand Canyon. Stay on Highway 180 to the 7.1 miles point *11.4 km* (MP 223) (2), then turn right on the Snow Bowl Road. Follow the Snow Bowl Road to the Sky Ride parking area at 14.2 miles *22.7 km.* Park there, 35°19.852'N, 111°42.378'W.

TRAILHEAD: You must buy a ticket and take the Sky Ride to the top. You can only take this hike in the months when the Sky Ride is open.

DESCRIPTION: We like to take a leisurely half day for this and our favorite time is in mid-October, when the aspen leaves are turning gold. We will often drive up, have lunch on the patio, then take the ride to the top, enjoying the superb views all along the way. We think that this is the best way to see the changing leaves in the fall, as you are treated to views that are simply unavailable any other way. You will see the ski runs carved out of the forest as you travel on the lift, and you can imagine what the ski conditions are like here in the winter.
    To make the hike, you get off at the end of the lift, 35°19.555'N, 111°41.084'W. Turn left and walk uphill. The trail is short and there is very little climb.
    The **Humphreys Trail** and the Lookout Trail are the only legal trails on this part of the mountain. There is no access to Agassiz Peak or Humphreys Peak from the Lookout Trail.
    Hours for the Skyride: Mid-June to Labor Day it runs 7 days a week, from 10:00 a.m. to 4:00 p.m. From Labor Day to Mid-October, it runs Friday, Saturday & Sunday only, from 10:00 a.m. to 4:00 p.m. The ride takes 30 minutes each way. Every rider must get off at the top.

Photo: This is one of the highest trails in the book, but you get there the easy way, on the Sky Ride. It is above timberline so you have unobstructed views.

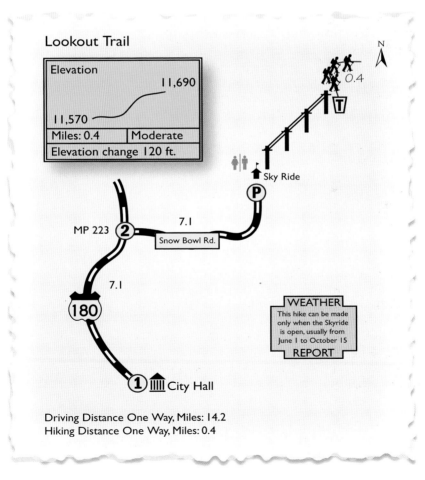

Lookout Trail

Elevation	
11,570 —	— 11,690
Miles: 0.4	Moderate
Elevation change 120 ft.	

N

0.4

Sky Ride

P

MP 223 (2)

7.1

Snow Bowl Rd.

7.1

(180)

WEATHER
This hike can be made only when the Skyride is open, usually from June 1 to October 15
REPORT

(1) City Hall

Driving Distance One Way, Miles: 14.2
Hiking Distance One Way, Miles: 0.4

McMillan Mesa Trail

Location Map D3
Flagstaff East, Flagstaff West USGS Maps
Flagstaff Trails Map©

Driving One-Way/Total: 2.7/5.4 mi. *4.3/8.6 km* (Time 10/20 minutes)
Access Road: All cars, All paved
Hiking One-Way/Total: 1.75/3.5 mi. *2.8/5.6 km* (Time 45/90 minutes)
How Strenuous: Easy   *Total Drive & Hike Time:* 1 hour 50 min.
Features: Flagstaff Urban Trail System hike, Easy to reach, Nice mesa with views over town

NUTSHELL: McMillan Mesa is an island between east and west Flagstaff. This trail takes you across the top of the mesa from south to north.

DIRECTIONS:
From Flagstaff City Hall (1) Go:
    East on Route 66 for 1.0 miles *1.6 km* to Switzer Canyon Road (2). Turn left (N) on Switzer Canyon Road and drive it to the 1.6 mile *2.6 km* point, where you turn right onto N. Turquoise Drive (3). Follow N. Turquoise Drive to the 1.9 mile *3.0 km* point, where you turn right onto E. Ponderosa Parkway (4). Follow E. Ponderosa Parkway to the 2.4 mile *3.8 km* point, where you turn left on N. Locust (5). At the 2.5 mile *4.0 km* point turn right on E. Apple (6). Follow E. Apple to the 2.6 mile *4.2 km* point, where you turn left on N. Hemlock (7). Take Hemlock to the 2.7 mile *4.3 km* point, where you will find a gravel parking place.

TRAILHEAD: At the parking place, 35°12.301'N 111°37.909'W.

DESCRIPTION: From the parking area you will make a gradual easy climb to the top of the mesa, heading east. The top of the mesa is a pleasant surprise. Although the town has built up around it, the city has owned McMillan Mesa for many years and most of it has been kept in pristine condition, with open grassy space in the middle of the mesa and trees around its perimeter.
    You will hike over to the eastern rim of the mesa and then turn north and walk along the rim. From here there are nice views of the San Francisco Peaks, the Dry Lake Hills and Mount Elden. You can look down onto sections of East Flagstaff.
    The trail proceeds northerly and is quite level, making an easy walk. Beyond the midpoint there are a few benches for sitting and enjoying the views. The trail passes a large materials dump and a power station and approaches Forest Drive, 35°12.895'N 111°37.864'W. We like to end by walking half way over the footbridge that spans Forest Drive.

Photo: This urban trail moves along the flank of a lovely meadow, which can be very pretty when wildflowers are in bloom in September.

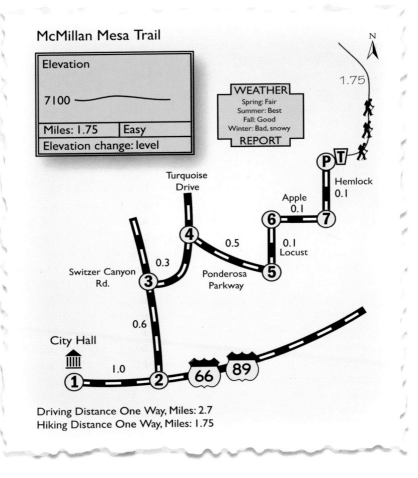

McMillan Mesa Trail

Elevation	
7100 ⌒	
Miles: 1.75	Easy
Elevation change: level	

WEATHER
Spring: Fair
Summer: Best
Fall: Good
Winter: Bad, snowy
REPORT

N

1.75

P T

Hemlock
0.1

Apple
0.1

Turquoise
Drive

6 ——— 7

④

0.5

0.1
Locust

0.3

Switzer Canyon
Rd.

③

Ponderosa
Parkway

⑤

0.6

City Hall

1.0

① ——— ② 66 89

Driving Distance One Way, Miles: 2.7
Hiking Distance One Way, Miles: 1.75

Mormon Mountain Trail #58

Location Map F5
Mormon Lake & Mormon Mountain USGS Maps
Coconino Forest Service Map

Driving One-Way/Total: 27.0/54.0 mi. *43.2/86.4 km* (Time 30/60 minutes)
Access Road: All cars, Last 0.3 miles *0.5 km* good gravel road
Hiking One-Way/Total: 3.0/6.0 mi. *4.8/9.6 km* (Time 2.0/4.0 hours)
How Strenuous: Hard   *Total Drive & Hike Time:* 5 hours
Features: Beautiful forest

NUTSHELL: This hike takes you to the top of the dominant mountain on the landscape 27.0 miles *43.2 km* southeast of Flagstaff.

DIRECTIONS:
From Flagstaff City Hall (1) Go:
   West, then south on Route 66 under the railroad overpass. At 0.5 miles *0.8 km*, leave Route 66 and go straight on Milton Road. See Access Map, page 10. At 1.7 miles *2.7 km* turn right at the light onto Forest Meadows Street. Go one block to Beulah. Turn left on Beulah and follow it south. Beulah merges onto Highway 89A. At 2.4 miles *3.8 km* (MP 401.6), turn left onto the Lake Mary Road (2). Follow the Lake Mary Road to the 23.0 mile *36.8 km* point (MP 323.6), where you turn right onto the Mormon Lake Road (Hwy 90) (3). At 26.7 miles *42.7 km*, turn right on the road to Dairy Springs (4). Follow the gravel road and signs to the parking area at the 27.0 mile *43.2 km* point, at the back of the Dairy Springs Campground, 34°57.298'N, 111°29.281'W.

TRAILHEAD: At the parking area.

DESCRIPTION: This trail is gentle and wide at the start, climbing through a lovely forest of pine, oak and fir, with some aspen and heavy brush near the top. The mid-part of the trail is very steep, then gentles out. As with many mountains, reaching the top is deceptive. You come to points where you clearly stop climbing and level out on what appears to be a crest only to find that it is merely a fold or a bench. This happens on this hike. You will not reach a point where you can definitely say to yourself, *"This is The Top."*
   One of the attractions of a mountain hike is being rewarded with great views at the summit. That does not happen here because the trees are so thick. You will emerge into a clearing where there is a trail sign, 34°57.713'N, 111°30.917'W. This is a good place to stop. You can turn left and walk up to the cinder road FR 648, about 0.1 miles *0.2 km*, and then turn left. From here you can walk down to the upper trailhead, a distance of 0.25 miles *0.4 km*, 34°57.575'N, 111°31.141'W.

Photo: Although this trail starts in a typical pine forest, the scenery changes as you climb. Extra moisture here creates a lush mix of trees and shrubs.

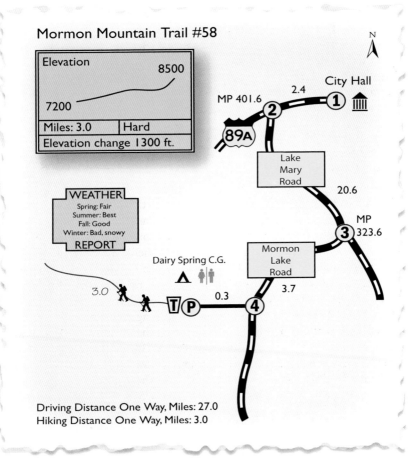

Mormon Mountain Trail #58

N

Elevation
8500
7200

Miles: 3.0	Hard
Elevation change 1300 ft.	

City Hall
2.4
MP 401.6 ② ① 🏛
89A

Lake
Mary
Road

20.6

MP
③ 323.6

WEATHER
Spring: Fair
Summer: Best
Fall: Good
Winter: Bad, snowy
REPORT

Mormon
Lake
Road

Dairy Spring C.G.
🏕 🚹🚺

3.0   0.3   3.7
T P ——— ④

Driving Distance One Way, Miles: 27.0
Hiking Distance One Way, Miles: 3.0

Museum Nature Trail

Location Map D3
Flagstaff West USGS Map
Coconino Forest Service Map

Driving One-Way/Total: 2.8/5.6 mi. *4.5/9.0 km* (Time 15/30 minutes)
Access Road: All cars, All paved
Hiking Distance, Complete Loop: 0.5 miles *0.8 km* (Time 30 minutes)
How Strenuous: Easy   *Total Drive & Hike Time:* 1 hour
Features: Beautiful nature trail on the campus of the Museum of Northern Arizona

NUTSHELL: This nature trail takes you down into a pretty canyon and along a streambed where many plants of the area grow.

DIRECTIONS:
From Flagstaff City Hall (1) Go:
   North on Humphreys Street a distance of 0.6 miles *1.0 km* to the light at Columbus (2). See Access Map, page 10. Turn left here onto Highway 180, the road to the Grand Canyon. At 2.8 miles *4.5 km* (MP 218.5) turn left into the entrance to The Museum of Northern Arizona (3). Park in the lot.

TRAILHEAD: To the left as you approach the main entrance to the museum. It is marked as the *Rio de Flag Nature Trail.* 35°14.048'N 111°39.930'W.

DESCRIPTION: At the beginning, you walk along the rim of a rock-walled canyon. Below is the Rio de Flag. The walls of the canyon here are about fifty feet high. You will come to a point where a flight of stone steps allows you to descend into the canyon easily. At the bottom, turn right.
   The streambed is overgrown with Arroyo Willows through most of the area. There is a little spring hidden in the willows, which flows in wet years and causes a stream to run along the bottom, an attractive feature.
   You hike along the north bank; then the trail meanders across the stream, crosses it on a plank bridge, and loops back to the south. At the point where you can go to your left across the creek and climb back to the top, take the right fork instead, on a short spur called The Aspen Trail. This takes you up a flight of stone steps to the top and over to a side canyon where a stand of aspens grows.
   From here the trail returns to the canyon floor and loops back to the trail junction, from where you go back to the trailhead on the first leg of the trail. Done this way, the hike is about 0.5 miles *0.8 km* long.

Photo: We like nature trails and we love the Museum of Northern Arizona, so this combination is a real winner.

Museum Nature Trail

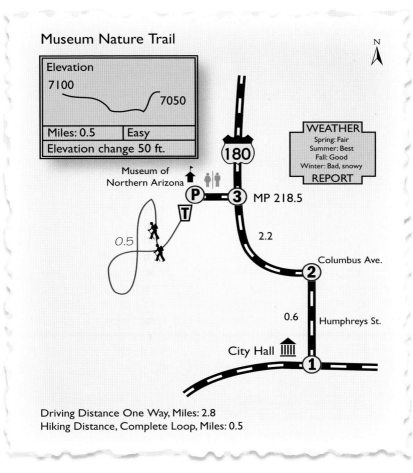

Elevation
7100
7050

| Miles: 0.5 | Easy |
| Elevation change 50 ft. | |

N

WEATHER
Spring: Fair
Summer: Best
Fall: Good
Winter: Bad, snowy
REPORT

180

Museum of
Northern Arizona

P   ③ MP 218.5
T

0.5

2.2

Columbus Ave.
②

0.6   Humphreys St.

City Hall

①

Driving Distance One Way, Miles: 2.8
Hiking Distance, Complete Loop, Miles: 0.5

Observatory Mesa Trail

Location Map D3
Flagstaff West USGS Map
Flagstaff Trails Map©

Driving One-Way/Total: 1.0/2.0 mi.*1.6/3.2 km* (Time 10/20 minutes)
Access Road: All cars, All paved
Hiking One-Way/Total: 1.6/3.2 mi. *2.6/5.1 km* (Time 50/100 minutes)
How Strenuous: Moderate   *Total Drive & Hike Time:* 2 hours
Features: Beautiful forest, Nicely maintained trail, Extremely easy access

NUTSHELL: This urban trail in west Flagstaff gives a moderate walk to the top of Observatory Mesa, the ridge that forms the town's western boundary.

DIRECTIONS:
From Flagstaff City Hall (1) Go:
    West on Route 66. Where Route 66 curves left under the overpass, go straight on Santa Fe Avenue. See Access Map, page 10. At 0.5 miles *0.8 km*, turn right on Thorpe Road (2). At 1.0 miles *1.6 km* you will see the trail by a stone hut to your left. There is no parking to the left. Turn right into a paved parking lot near the ball fields (3). Park there. 35°12.428'N 111°39.463'W. [At press time there was construction work at the site, which may change the parking situation].

TRAILHEAD: Walk across Thorpe Road. You will see a trail sign in front of the stone building. 35°12.438'N 111°39.541'W.

DESCRIPTION: This Flagstaff Urban Trail uses part of the old road to Lowell Observatory. It is surfaced with cinders and kept in good condition. It is heavily used by hikers, runners and bikers.
    You will walk up a little canyon that is pleasant and peaceful with a nice stand of big old pine trees on a mild grade at first.
    At 0.7 miles *1.1 km* you reach a point where the old road to Lowell Observatory turned left. 35°12.599'N 111°40.064'W. You can see rock work that supported the road. Go straight ahead. You will climb some more, on a steeper grade, to the 0.8 mile *1.3 km* point, where you top out. From there the trail is level to the end, running westerly, on a nice level stretch. The trail terminates at a road junction at 1.6 miles *2.6 km*. 35°12.595'N 111°41.015'W. Bikers use this as access to the miles of forest roads that cross the mesa, but don't try to hike them unless you have a map. It's easy to get lost on foot.
    The old road was built by the Town of Flagstaff about 1894 as an inducement to get Dr. Percival Lowell to locate his observatory here. Lowell was given his pick of ten acres of land free and the town promised to build a road to the site. Lowell selected land at the top of the hill and the town built this road.

Photo: We consider this to be one of the best of the Flagstaff Urban Trails, as it offers an interesting and moderately challenging hike.

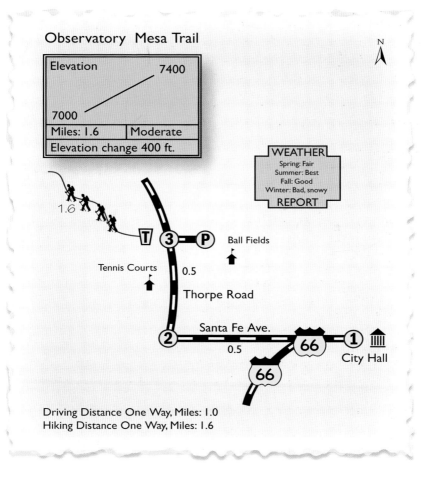

Observatory Mesa Trail

N

Elevation	
7400	
7000	
Miles: 1.6	Moderate
Elevation change 400 ft.	

WEATHER
Spring: Fair
Summer: Best
Fall: Good
Winter: Bad, snowy
REPORT

1.6

T 3 P Ball Fields

Tennis Courts 0.5

Thorpe Road

Santa Fe Ave.
2 66 1 City Hall
0.5
66

Driving Distance One Way, Miles: 1.0
Hiking Distance One Way, Miles: 1.6

Old Caves Crater

Location Map D4
Sunset Crater West USGS Map
Flagstaff Trails Map©

Driving One-Way/Total: 8.8/17.6 mi. *14.1/28.2 km* (Time 20/40 minutes)
Access Road: All cars, All paved
Hiking One-Way/Total: 1.3/2.6 mi. *2.1/4.2 km* (Time 30/60 minutes)
How Strenuous: Moderate   *Total Drive & Hike Time:* 1 hour 40 min.
Features: Indian ruins, Strange volcanic caves

NUTSHELL: Old Caves Crater is a cinder hill located east of Flagstaff. On top are a fascinating series of natural caves that were used as dwellings by the ancient Native Americans whom we call the Sinaguans.

DIRECTIONS:
From Flagstaff City Hall (1) Go:
   East, then north on Highway 89 for 8.3 miles *13.3 km*, to the Silver Saddle Road (stoplight) (2). Turn right on Silver Saddle and drive to the 8.8 mile *14.1 km* point (3), where you turn left into the parking lot.

TRAILHEAD: At the parking lot, 35°16.217'N, 111°32.146'W.

DESCRIPTION: Old Caves Crater has been known since the first Anglo settlers came into Flagstaff, but it has not received much publicity. This is hard to understand, because it is a fascinating site.
   The trail is a blend of old roads and footpaths, taking you up the south face of the crater. On top you will emerge onto a saddle between two knobs 35°16.724'N, 111°31.717'W. Turn right and walk a short distance and you will find a number of caves that appear to have been formed by gas bubbles passing through red lava, 35°16.690'N, 111°31.760'W. These bubbles formed hollows and then burst in such a way that openings to the caves were created. The ancients used these natural shelters as dwellings. They have been filled in to a great extent so that it is difficult to see the shelters today, but in the past this was the home of a small community.
   The site has been thoroughly pothunted. This digging and natural rockfalls have closed the entrances to several of the caves. This was a major Sinagua pueblo, occupied about 1200 A.D.
   From the saddle you will find a footpath over to the higher north knob of the crater. It is an easy 0.2 mile *0.3 km* walk, worth doing to enjoy the views.
   There is another access from the road to the city landfill but we think that it is not as good as this one.

Photo: A series of volcanic blow holes such as the one seen here, once furnished shelter to the Sinaguas.

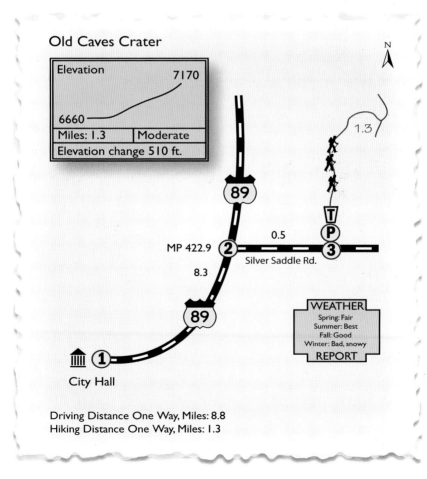

Old Caves Crater

Elevation		
		7170
6660		
Miles: 1.3	Moderate	
Elevation change 510 ft.		

N

89

1.3

MP 422.9 **2** — 0.5 — **3**
Silver Saddle Rd.

T
P

8.3

89

WEATHER
Spring: Fair
Summer: Best
Fall: Good
Winter: Bad, snowy
REPORT

1
City Hall

Driving Distance One Way, Miles: 8.8
Hiking Distance One Way, Miles: 1.3

Oldham Trail #1

Location Map D4
Flagstaff East & West, Humphreys Peak & Sunset Crater W. USGS Maps
Flagstaff Trails Map©

Driving One-Way/Total: 2.3/4.6 mi. *3.7/7.4 km* (Time 10/20 minutes)
Access Road: All cars, All paved
Hiking One-Way/Total: 3.2/6.4 mi. *5.1/10.2 km* (Time 1.5/3.0 hours)
How Strenuous: Moderate   *Total Drive & Hike Time:* 3 hours 20 min.
Features: Views

NUTSHELL: This trail is part of the Mt. Elden trail system, taking you from Buffalo Park through a beautiful forest.

DIRECTIONS:
From Flagstaff City Hall (1) Go:
    North on Humphreys Street to the stoplight at 0.6 miles *1.0 km*. See Access Map, page 10. Turn right here onto Columbus Avenue and go one block east to the next stop sign, at Beaver Street. Turn left onto Beaver Street and go up the hill. At the 1.0 mile *1.6 km* point turn right on Forest Avenue. On top of the hill, at 1.9 miles *3.0 km*, turn left on Gemini Drive. At 2.3 miles *3.7 km* you want to park in the lot for **Buffalo Park**, 35°13.054'N, 111°37.977'W.

TRAILHEAD: At the far end of the park, 35°13.523'N, 111°37.855'W.

DESCRIPTION: Walk the central **Utilities Access Trail** for 0.5 miles *0.8 km* to the fence, where the Oldham Trail #1 starts. You will walk a rocky stretch downhill into a canyon bottom, taking the right fork at the first trail junction there.
    Then the trail rises and at 1.4 miles *2.2 km* you will reach the junction of Oldham Trail #1 and the **Pipeline Trail**, 35°14.079'N, 111°37.679'W. Turn left
    From this junction the trail becomes harder (steep) but more interesting as you hike through stands of oak, aspen, fir and spruce. Lava cliffs and groups of boulders big as boxcars that have tumbled from the cliffs of Mt. Elden add visual interest.
    The Oldham Trail ends at 3.2 miles *5.1 km*, where it meets the Elden Lookout Road, FR 557, at 35°13.523'N, 111°37.855'W, where there is a small parking area.
    A nice way to enjoy this hike is to use two cars. Take both to Buffalo Park. Then everybody gets into one of the cars and drives it to the parking area mentioned above, a point 2.6 miles *4.2 km* up the Elden Lookout Road. This way you hike mostly downhill.

Photo: Being able to walk alongside giant lava boulders and cliffs is one of the most attractive features of this trail.

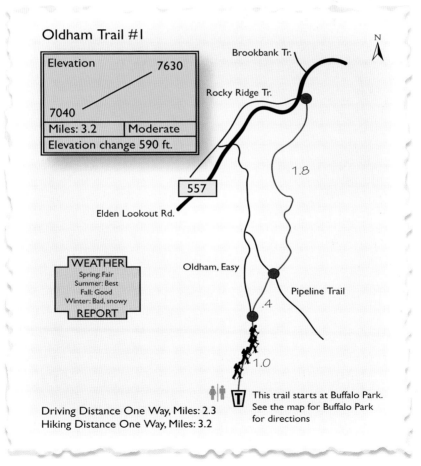

Oldham Trail #1

Elevation		7630
7040		
Miles: 3.2	Moderate	
Elevation change 590 ft.		

Brookbank Tr.

Rocky Ridge Tr.

N

557

Elden Lookout Rd.

1.8

WEATHER
Spring: Fair
Summer: Best
Fall: Good
Winter: Bad, snowy
REPORT

Oldham, Easy

Pipeline Trail

.4

1.0

This trail starts at Buffalo Park.
See the map for Buffalo Park
for directions

Driving Distance One Way, Miles: 2.3
Hiking Distance One Way, Miles: 3.2

Oldham Trail, Easy

Location Map D4
Flagstaff East & West, Humphreys Peak &
Sunset Crater W. USGS Maps
Flagstaff Trails Map©

Driving One-Way/Total: 2.3/4.6 mi. *3.7/7.4 km* (Time 10/20 minutes)
Access Road: All cars, All paved
Hiking One-Way/Total: 2.5/5.0 mi. *4.0/8.0 km* (Time 1.0/2.0 hours)
How Strenuous: Moderate   *Total Drive & Hike Time:* 2 hours 20 min.
Features: Views

NUTSHELL: This trail is part of the Mt. Elden trail system, taking you from Buffalo Park through a beautiful forest.

DIRECTIONS:
From Flagstaff City Hall (1) Go:
    North on Humphreys Street to the stoplight at 0.6 miles *1.0 km*. See Access Map, page 10. Turn right here onto Columbus Avenue and go one block east to the next stop sign, at Beaver Street. Turn left onto Beaver Street and go up the hill. At the 1.0 mile *1.6 km* point turn right on Forest Avenue. On top of the hill, at 1.9 miles *3.0 km*, turn left on Gemini Drive. At 2.3 miles *3.7 km* you want to park in the lot for **Buffalo Park**, 35°13.054'N, 111°37.977'W.

TRAILHEAD: At the far end of the park, 35°13.523'N, 111°37.855'W.

DESCRIPTION: Walk the central **Utilities Access Trail** for 0.5 miles *0.8 km* to the fence, where the Oldham Trail #1 starts. You will walk a rocky stretch downhill into a canyon bottom, taking the left fork at the first trail junction there.
    Then the trail rises and at 1.7 miles *2.7 km* you will reach the junction of the Easy Oldham Trail and the **Pipeline Trail**, 35°14.386'N, 111°37.875'W. Go straight.
    This trail lives up to its name, being easier than the **Oldham Trail #1**, but it is not as interesting, just a nice ramble through the woods with nothing exciting in the way of scenery.
    The Easy Oldham Trail ends at 2.5 miles *4.0 km*, where it meets the Elden Lookout Road, FR 557, at 35°14.973'N, 111°38.028'W, where there is a small parking area.
    The mountain bikers of Flagstaff love this network of trails and you are likely to meet one or more during your hike. Their greater range allows them to mix and match the trails, but for a hiker it is better to go out and back on the same trail here.

Photo: The system of trails of which this trail is a part, are popular with Flagstaff residents: easy to reach, not too strenuous, and scenic.

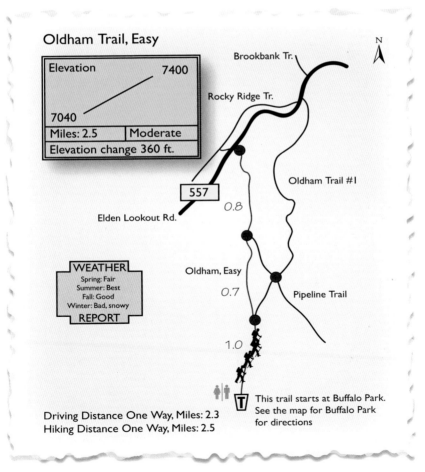

Oldham Trail, Easy

Elevation		7400
7040		
Miles: 2.5	Moderate	
Elevation change 360 ft.		

N

Brookbank Tr.

Rocky Ridge Tr.

Oldham Trail #1

557

Elden Lookout Rd.

0.8

WEATHER
Spring: Fair
Summer: Best
Fall: Good
Winter: Bad, snowy
REPORT

Oldham, Easy

0.7

Pipeline Trail

1.0

This trail starts at Buffalo Park.
See the map for Buffalo Park
for directions

Driving Distance One Way, Miles: 2.3
Hiking Distance One Way, Miles: 2.5

Oldham Trail, Upper

Location Map D4
Humphreys Peak & Sunset Crater West USGS Maps
Flagstaff Trails Map©

Driving One-Way/Total: 7.0/14.0 mi. *11.2/22.4 km* (Time 30/60 minutes)
Access Road: All cars, Last 2.4 miles *3.8 km* medium unpaved road
Hiking One-Way/Total: 2.2/4.4 mi. *3.5/7.0 km* (Time 1.5/3.0 hours)
How Strenuous: Hard   *Total Drive & Hike Time:* 4.0 hours
Features: Views, Forests

NUTSHELL: This trail, part of the Dry Lake Hills/Mt. Elden system, starts at a point on the Elden Lookout Road and makes a steep climb up Mt. Elden to Sunset Park.

DIRECTIONS:
From Flagstaff City Hall (1) Go:
   North on Humphreys Street for 0.6 miles *1.0 km*. See Access Map, page 10. Turn left at the light onto Highway 180, the Grand Canyon Road. At 3.1 miles *5.0 km* (MP 218.6), turn right on the Schultz Pass Road, FR 420 (2). At 3.6 miles *5.8 km* go straight ahead on the Elden Lookout Road (FR 557). Follow FR 557 to the 7.0 mile *11.2 km* point, where you turn right into a small parking lot, 35°15.281'N, 111°37.493'W.

TRAILHEAD: At the parking place, signed.

DESCRIPTION: At the trailhead turn left and follow an old road for the first part of the trail. The climb on this stretch of the trail is gradual and doesn't really prepare you for the steep climb that is to follow. This early part of the trail takes you through a dense spruce forest.
   The old road ends where it bumps up against the flank of Mt. Elden. From there the trail is a footpath climbing the mountain. This second part of the trail is very steep, really a hard climb. It also passes through a heavy forest. The trees are so thick that you don't get many views.
   Near the end of the trail you come out into an open meadow, Oldham Park. You cross it and reach the Elden Lookout Road at a small parking area, 35°15.216'N, 111°36.217'W. Go across the Elden Lookout Road up to the skyline where you will see trail signs. The trail ends where it intersects the **Sunset Trail**. 35°15.231'N, 111°36.174'W. You can walk along the crest in either direction to enjoy the views, which are unobstructed by timber due to the Radio Fire that burned away many acres of timber in June 1977.

Photo: Dick has reached the top of the trail and is about to enter Oldham Park an open grassy meadow, glimpsed here.

Oldham Trail, Upper

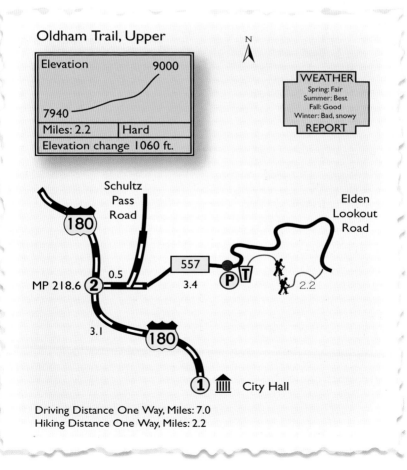

Elevation	9000
7940	
Miles: 2.2	Hard
Elevation change 1060 ft.	

N

WEATHER
Spring: Fair
Summer: Best
Fall: Good
Winter: Bad, snowy
REPORT

Schultz Pass Road

180

Elden Lookout Road

557

MP 218.6 **2**

0.5

3.4

P T

2.2

3.1

180

1 🏛 City Hall

Driving Distance One Way, Miles: 7.0
Hiking Distance One Way, Miles: 2.2

Pipeline Trail #42

Location Map D4
Flagstaff East and Flagstaff West USGS Maps
Flagstaff Trails Map©

Driving One-Way/Total: 5.2/10.4 mi. *8.3/16.6 km* (Time 15/30 minutes)
Access Road: All cars, All paved
Hiking One-Way/Total: 4.2/8.4 mi. *6.7/13.4 km* (Time 2.0/4.0 hours)
How Strenuous: Moderate   *Total Drive & Hike Time:* 4.5 hours
Features: Views, Connections to other trails

NUTSHELL: Located just north of Flagstaff, this moderate hike takes you around the base of Mt. Elden to connect with the Elden Lookout trailhead in East Flagstaff.

DIRECTIONS:
From Flagstaff City Hall (1) Go:
   East, then north on Highway 89. See Access Map, pages 10-11. At 5.2 miles *8.3 km* (MP 419.5) just past the Flagstaff Mall, you will see a trailhead sign and a paved driveway to your left into a parking lot bounded by a pole fence (2). Pull in there and park, 35°13.812'N 111°34.762'W.

TRAILHEAD: Hike up the Fat Man's Trail for 0.2 miles *0.3 km* and take the left trail fork. At 0.5 miles *0.8 km* you will reach the Pipeline trailhead, 35°14.058'N 111°35.102'W.

DESCRIPTION: The trail runs along the natural gas pipeline where it can, but there are places where access to it is blocked, in which case you are diverted into the forest. At the start you will hike through the woods for a while until you reach a place where the trail turns left, 35°13.635'N, 111°35.491'W and goes down to the pipeline road, meeting it at 35°13.582'N, 111°35.511'W.
   From this point you will hike the actual pipeline about 1.0 mile *1.6 km* and then turn right, up into the woods again, at 35°13.525'N, 111°36.481'W as you pass a blocked spot. Look carefully for the trail marker as you go uphill, and then turn left again, at 35°13.610'N, 111°36.483'W. You will hike a nice forest trail for a while and then turn left down to the Pipeline Road again—watch for markers.
   At 3.8 miles *6.1 km* you will meet **Oldham Trail #1** coming up out of **Buffalo Park**, 35°14.079'N, 111°37.679'W. Turn right and go to the 4.2 mile *6.7 km* point, the official end of Pipeline Trail, where it meets the **Oldham, Easy Trail**. *2-car Shortcut:* at X (map) it is 1.4 miles *2.2 km* to the parking lot at Buffalo Park, 35°13.054'N, 111°37.977'W. To use two cars, leave one at Buffalo Park and take the other to the Pipeline Trailhead.

Photo: Our favorite parts of this trail are those that move through or near the interesting lava formations found on the side of Mt. Elden.

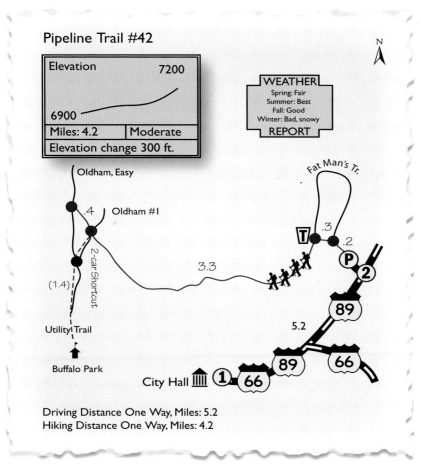

Pipeline Trail #42

N

Elevation	7200
6900	
Miles: 4.2	Moderate
Elevation change 300 ft.	

WEATHER
Spring: Fair
Summer: Best
Fall: Good
Winter: Bad, snowy
REPORT

Fat Man's Tr.

Oldham, Easy

.4 Oldham #1

.3

T .2

P

2-car Shortcut

3.3

2

89

(1.4)

5.2

Utility Trail

89 66

Buffalo Park

City Hall 1 66

Driving Distance One Way, Miles: 5.2
Hiking Distance One Way, Miles: 4.2

Priest Draw Trail

Location Map E4
Lower Lake Mary USGS Map
Coconino Forest Service Map

Driving One-Way/Total: 11.4/22.8 mi. *18.2/36.5 km* (Time 30/60 minutes)
Access Road: All cars, Last 3.0 miles *4.8 km* good gravel roads
Hiking One-Way/Total: 1.5/3.0 mi. 2.4/4.8 *km* (Time 45/90 minutes)
How Strenuous: Easy   *Total Drive & Hike Time:* 2 hours 30 min.
Features: Beautiful canyon, Rock climbing area, Easy to reach

NUTSHELL: An easy drive south of Flagstaff, this trail passes through part of Priest Draw, a shallow canyon lined with limestone walls.

DIRECTIONS:
From Flagstaff City Hall (1) Go:
West and then south (left) on Route 66 under the railroad overpass. See Access Map, page 10. At 0.5 miles *0.8 km*, go straight on Milton Road. At 1.7 miles *2.7 km* turn right at the light at Forest Meadows. At the next corner turn left on Beulah and follow it out of town. Beulah connects onto Highway 89A. At 2.4 miles *3.8 km* (MP 401.6) turn left on the Lake Mary Road (2). Follow the Lake Mary Road to the 8.1 mile *13.0 km* point, then turn right on Crimson Road (3). It almost immediately feeds onto Lockett (County Hwy 132). The paving soon ends, giving way to good gravel roads. Stay on this to the 11.1 mile *17.8 km* point, and then turn right on a dirt road (4). Drive to the 11.4 point *18.2 km*, the parking lot, 35°04.881'N, 111°36.060'W.

TRAILHEAD: At the parking lot.

DESCRIPTION: You will walk across a wash to the north side of the canyon and stay there for the entire trail.
There are picturesque white limestone walls lining the canyon, and you may find what appear to be very large bats hanging from the underside of undercut shelves. Actually these are human rock climbers who love this area as a favorite site for their special kind of rock climbing.
The trail does not do anything special, it just moves along the canyon. The best thing about the trail is the limestone. We really enjoy walking near and in some cases through the colorful and pockmarked cliffs and boulders.
The trail ends at another parking place that looks very much like the first, marked by a pole fence, 35°04.665'N, 111°37.418'W. You could go out past this place and hike the road, but there isn't much point in doing so. The canyon widens here and the limestone disappears.

Photo: Although Flagstaff's many extinct volcanoes and their lava flows and cinders are most prominent, there is plenty of limestone too, as seen here.

Priest Draw

N
↑

Elevation	
6950 ⎯⎯⎯⎯⎯⎯ 6650	
Miles: 1.5	Easy
Elevation change 300 ft.	

WEATHER
Spring: Fair
Summer: Best
Fall: Good
Winter: Bad, snowy
REPORT

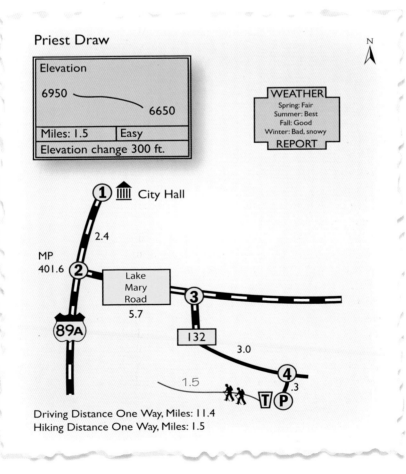

(1) 🏛 City Hall

2.4

MP
401.6 (2)

Lake
Mary
Road
5.7

(3)

132

3.0

(4)
.3

1.5

🚶🚶 T P

Driving Distance One Way, Miles: 11.4
Hiking Distance One Way, Miles: 1.5

89A

Pumpkin Trail #39

Location Map C2
Kendrick Peak, Moritz Ridge and Wing Mt. USGS Maps
Kaibab Forest Service Map

Driving One-Way/Total: 25.2/50.4 mi. *40.3/80.6 km* (Time 1.0/2.0 hours)
Access Road: All cars, Last 11.1 miles *17.8 km* fair gravel road
Hiking One-Way/Total: 5.5/11.0 mi. *8.8/17.6 km* (Time 3.0/6.0 hours)
How Strenuous: Hard   *Total Drive & Hike Time:* 8 hours
Features: Ten thousand foot peak, Views

NUTSHELL: This trail winds to the summit of 10, 418-foot Kendrick Peak.

DIRECTIONS:
From Flagstaff City Hall (1) Go:
   North on Humphreys Street for 0.6 miles *1.0 km*. See Access Map, page 10.
Turn left at the light onto Highway 180 the Grand Canyon Road. At 14.1 miles
22.6 km (MP 230.1) (2) turn left on gravel road, FR 245. Follow it to the 17.1 mile
27.4 km point where it intersects FR 171 (3). Turn right on FR 171 and follow it to
the 24.3 mile *38.9 km* point, where you will see a sign for the Pumpkin Trail (4).
Turn right and drive to the trailhead, which you will reach at 25.2 miles *40.3 km*.
Park in the parking area.

TRAILHEAD: At the parking area. 35°25.383'N, 111°53.861'W.

DESCRIPTION: Unlike the nearby **Kendrick Mt. Trail**, which was made to
provide access to a fire lookout tower by the Forest Service, the Pumpkin Trail
seems to have been built by and for sheepherders haphazardly. It is rough and has
some very steep grades.
   You will climb along the side of a canyon for 1.0 miles *1.6 km* to a fence. Here
you will turn right and begin going up a ridge. At 1.4 miles *2.2 km* you will meet
the Connector Trail coming over from the **Bull Basin Trail.**
   You will see extensive damage caused by the 2000 forest fire. The trail gets
very rocky and rough. At about 3.0 miles *4.8 km* you will find breaks in the forests
punctuated by meadows. The meadows provide good viewpoints.
   From the 4.0 mile *6.4 km* point the trail gets really steep and is hard going. You
will reach the burnt ruins of a log cabin at 5.0 miles *8.0 km* located at the edge
of the biggest meadow. The slope of this meadow falls away so steeply that they
must have issued spiked shoes to the sheep.
   Beyond this meadow the trail is primitive and harder, clawing its way to the
top just below the base of the lookout tower at 5.5 miles *8.8 km*. 35°24.476'N
111°51.009'W. Don't count on being allowed to climb up into the tower.

---

*Photo: This is a little-used trail up the side of Kendrick Mountain. Part of it
runs through an area burned in 2000, leading to fallen timbers, like this one.*

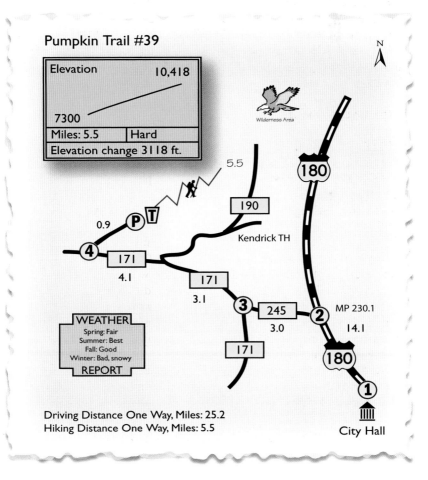

Pumpkin Trail #39

N

Elevation	10,418
7300	
Miles: 5.5	Hard
Elevation change 3118 ft.	

Wilderness Area

5.5

180

190

Kendrick TH

0.9 P T

4

171

4.1

171

3.1

3

245

3.0

2 MP 230.1

14.1

180

WEATHER
Spring: Fair
Summer: Best
Fall: Good
Winter: Bad, snowy
REPORT

171

1

City Hall

Driving Distance One Way, Miles: 25.2
Hiking Distance One Way, Miles: 5.5

Railroad Tunnel Trail

Location Map F5
Dane Canyon, Kehl Ridge USGS Maps
Coconino Forest Service Map

Driving One-Way/Total: 78.0/156.0 mi. *124.8/249.6 km* (Time 2.5/5.0 hours)
Access Road: All cars, Last 12.2 miles *19.5 km* good dirt road
Hiking One-Way/Total: 0.6/1.2 mi. *1.0/1.9 km* (40/80 minutes)
How Strenuous: Moderate   *Total Drive & Hike Time:* 6 hours 20 min.
Features: Beautiful Mogollon Rim, Historic railroad tunnel

NUTSHELL: After enjoying a portion of the Rim Drive, you will hike to a historic relic, a railroad tunnel boring into the side of the Mogollon Rim.

DIRECTIONS:
From Flagstaff City Hall (1) Go:
West, then south on Route 66, under the railroad overpass. At 0.5 miles *0.8 km*, go straight on Milton Road. See Access Map, page 10. At 1.7 miles *2.7 km* turn right on Forest Meadows, go one block and turn left on Beulah and follow it south as it merges onto Hwy 89A. At 2.4 miles *3.8 km* (MP 401.6), turn left on the Lake Mary Road (2). Drive Lake Mary Road (FH 3) to its end, where it meets State Route 87, 56.6 miles *90.6 km* (3). Turn right on Hwy 87, a paved road, and go to the 65.8 mile *105.3 km* point MP 280, where you turn left on FR 300 a good gravel road (4). Follow it to the 78.0 mile *124.8 km* point, the monument to the Battle of Big Dry Wash. Park near the monument, 34°27.254'N, 111°15.039'W.

TRAILHEAD: Across the road from the battle monument.

DESCRIPTION: The trail runs beneath the power line. Leave the power line at the second pole and move to your left, where you will walk an old road used in tunnel construction. The trail goes down 0.33 miles *0.5 km*, and then makes a sharp left turn, hooking uphill. It goes up 0.25 miles *0.4 km* to the tunnel, on a scenic shelf of land, 34°26.974'N, 111°14.865'W.

The first reaction of any visitor is to ask, "Why in the world was this built?" The tunnel was part of an 1885 plan to build a railroad from Flagstaff to Globe. Rim area residents were recruited to dig this tunnel in advance of the rails, taking their wages in stock certificates instead of cash. The railroad went bankrupt and was abandoned, leaving this tunnel high and dry, miles away from anything, the sorrowful crews holding worthless paper.

To make the Rim Drive, go east on FR 300. The drive is 34.5 miles *55.2 km*. It ends at paved Highway 260, where you turn right and go to Payson. From Payson you can return to Flagstaff via Camp Verde or on Highway 87. Takes a full day.

Photo: There is nothing like it in northern Arizona. This tunnel runs some 70 feet into the mountain and stops. It's a fascinating sight in a pretty place.

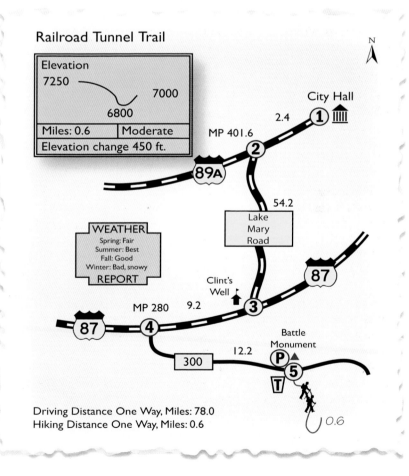

Railroad Tunnel Trail

Elevation
7250
7000
6800
Miles: 0.6 | Moderate
Elevation change 450 ft.

N

City Hall
2.4 ⓵ 🏛

MP 401.6
⓶
89A

54.2
Lake
Mary
Road

87

WEATHER
Spring: Fair
Summer: Best
Fall: Good
Winter: Bad, snowy
REPORT

Clint's
Well
MP 280   9.2   ⓷

87   ⓸

300   12.2   Battle
Monument
P ▲
T ⓹

0.6

Driving Distance One Way, Miles: 78.0
Hiking Distance One Way, Miles: 0.6

Red Mountain

Location Map B2
Chapel Mountain USGS Map
Coconino Forest Service Map

Driving One-Way/Total: 30.9/61.8 mi. *49.4/98.9 km* (Time 40/80 minutes)
Access Road: All cars, Last 0.3 miles *0.5 km* good gravel road
Hiking One-Way/Total: 1.5/3.0 mi. *2.4/4.8 km* (Time 45/90 minutes)
How Strenuous: Moderate   *Total Drive & Hike Time:* 2 hours 50 min.
Features: Unique experience—you go into the heart of a cutaway volcano

NUTSHELL: This magic hike takes you into the heart of Red Mountain to enjoy its otherworldly sculptures and formations. **A personal favorite.**

DIRECTIONS:
From Flagstaff City Hall (1) Go:
   North on Humphreys Street 0.6 miles *1.0 km*. See Access Map, page 10. Turn left on Columbus Avenue. It makes a big curve to the north and turns into Highway 180. Drive Highway 180 to the 30.6 miles *49.0 km* point (MP 247)(2), then turn left on an unpaved road. You will see a sign reading, "Red Mountain Trailhead" just before you get there. Drive to the 30.9 mile *49.4 km* point, where there is a parking lot.

TRAILHEAD: The trailhead is at the parking lot, 35°32.225'N, 111°51.490'W.

DESCRIPTION: Your objective will have been in sight for miles. Red Mountain looks just like hundreds of other cinder hills in the area north of Flagstaff except for one thing: its east face is sheared off cleanly, as if someone had done a cross-section of it to expose its red innards.
   This is piñon-juniper country and the land is pretty flat. It is an easy walk on a closed road though the trail rises constantly. At 0.75 miles *1.2 km* the trail leaves the old road it has been following and goes into the bed of a wash. This makes for fine walking as the bed is hard sand, and it makes a perfect entrance into Red Mountain. As you come nearer, the streambed becomes the bottom of a V flanked by high black cinder shoulders. Then you see strange black lava formations forming a sort of gate at the entrance to the insides of the mountain.
   At the 1.2 mile *1.9 km* point, you climb stairs and enter the interior of the crater, surrounded by weird hoodoos. The place is like a mini-Bryce Canyon.
   The trail continues up the wash, ending at 35°31.680'N, 111°52.395'W. From here you can explore all around, enjoying the colors, shapes, play of light and other features that make this place so special. Everywhere you look there is something to delight your eye.

Photo: Dick is just about to go into the center of the mountain here, through a narrow gorge formed by steep banks of black cinder. A magic place.

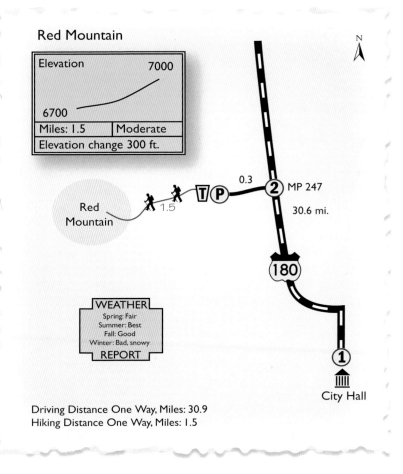

Red Mountain

Elevation	7000
6700	
Miles: 1.5	Moderate
Elevation change 300 ft.	

N

Red Mountain — 1.5 — T P — 0.3 — ② MP 247

30.6 mi.

180

WEATHER
Spring: Fair
Summer: Best
Fall: Good
Winter: Bad, snowy
REPORT

①
City Hall

Driving Distance One Way, Miles: 30.9
Hiking Distance One Way, Miles: 1.5

Rio de Flag Trail

Location Map D3
Flagstaff West USGS Map
Flagstaff Trails Map©

Driving One-Way/Total: 1.0/2.0 mi. *1.6/3.2 km* (Time 10/20 minutes)
Access Road: All cars, All paved
Hiking One-Way/Total: 1.0/2.0 mi. *1.6/3.2 km* (Time 30/60 minutes)
How Strenuous: Easy *Total Drive & Hike Time:* 1 hour 20 min.
Features: Urban trail, Bird-watching wetland

NUTSHELL: This urban trail in south Flagstaff follows the Rio de Flag from Sawmill Park east to the I-40 underpass.

DIRECTIONS:
From Flagstaff City Hall (1) Go:
    East on Route 66 for one block to Beaver Street (2). Turn right and go south four blocks to Butler Avenue (stoplight) (3). Turn left on Butler Avenue and drive east for five blocks to Lone Tree Road (stoplight) (4). Turn right on Lone Tree Street and follow it two blocks south, then turn left onto Sawmill Road (5) and follow the signs to Sawmill Park 35°11.324'N 111°38.627'W.

TRAILHEAD: Located on the west side of the park's playground equipment 35°11.306'N 111°38.710'W.

DESCRIPTION: The Rio de Flag Trail is part of the Flagstaff Urban Trail System (FUTS).
    You hike downhill to join the main trail in the canyon bottom, and then turn left. The trail follows along the course of the Rio de Flag. The grade is built up and the riverbed has been banked and channeled so that the trail should stay dry except in major floods. The path is the width of a single-lane road and it has been graded and surfaced so that the footing is very good.
    This is an urban trail and you are surrounded by industry on the north and residences on the south, but the canyon is deep enough so that you don't see too much of this and in places it feels as if you are out in the country. Reclaimed sewer water runs in the streambed near the end of the trail and forms a marsh, which is an excellent place for bird watching.
    At the end of the hike you are jarred when you come out of the canyon under the roaring traffic of Interstate-40 on two bridges overhead at the 1.0 mile *1.6 km* point. Just beyond the second bridge is a sewage treatment plant with a lake. We stop here, 35°11.055'N, 111°37.961'W. On the other side of the lake you will see a portion of the **Arizona Trail** marked by a little sign.

Photo: This urban trail is flat but it goes along the floor of an interesting canyon with limestone ledges and a sometimes large pond.

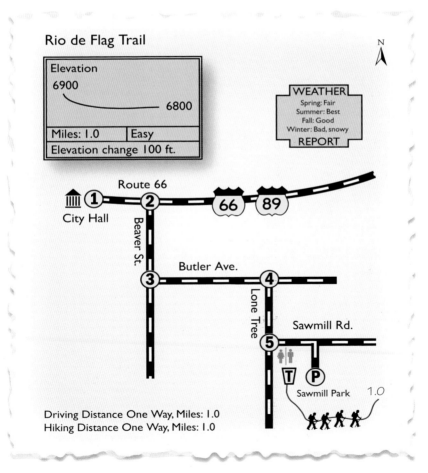

Rio de Flag Trail

N

Elevation	
6900	
	6800
Miles: 1.0	Easy
Elevation change 100 ft.	

WEATHER
Spring: Fair
Summer: Best
Fall: Good
Winter: Bad, snowy
REPORT

Route 66

1 City Hall

2

66 **89**

Beaver St.

Butler Ave.

3 **4**

Lone Tree

Sawmill Rd.

5

T P

Sawmill Park   1.0

Driving Distance One Way, Miles: 1.0
Hiking Distance One Way, Miles: 1.0

Rocky Ridge Trail #153

Location Map D4
Flagstaff West, Humphreys Peak & Sunset Crater West USGS Maps
Flagstaff Trails Map©

Driving One-Way/Total: 3.9/7.8 mi. *6.2/12.5 km* (Time 20/40 minutes)
Access Road: All cars, Last 0.25 miles *0.4 km* medium gravel road
Hiking One-Way/Total: 2.8/5.6 mi. *4.5/9.0 km* (Time 1.5/3.0 hours)
How Strenuous: Moderate   *Total Drive & Hike Time:* 3 hours 40 min.
Features: Shady forest in the hills north of town

NUTSHELL: This trail hugs the base of the south face of the Dry Lake Hills about 4.0 miles *6.4 km* north of Flagstaff and goes from the Schultz Pass Road to the Elden Lookout Road.

DIRECTIONS:
From Flagstaff City Hall (1) Go:
    North on Humphreys Street for 0.6 miles *1.0 km*. See Access Map, page 10. Turn left at the light onto Highway 180, the Grand Canyon Road. At 3.1 miles *5.0 km* (MP 218.6), turn right on the Schultz Pass Road, FR 420 (2). Stay on the Schultz Pass Road, curving left. At the 3.9 miles *6.2 km* point, you will see a gate, which closes the road in winter. Just beyond the gate is FR 9128Y which goes downhill to your right (3). Take this. At the bottom turn left and follow the road a few yards to a fence. Park nearby 35°14.709'N 111°39.678'W.

TRAILHEAD: Marked with a sign at the parking place. Same GPS reading.

DESCRIPTION: This trail starts where the **Schultz Creek Trail** ends. Both are signed.
    The Rocky Ridge Trail climbs about 300 feet and then stays fairly level. You will walk through a forest so thick that you have only a few views. You can see Buffalo Park and the NAU campus clearly, but most of Flagstaff is below a mesa that cuts off your view of the town.
    The trail takes you around the toe of the Dry Lake Hills and then follows along their south face. From the 1.0 mile *1.6 km* point onward you will be aware that the Elden Lookout Road is nearby on your right. Sometimes you can only hear sounds coming from it, while in other places you can see the road and will be a stone's throw from it. Mountain bikers love the road and many of them use the Rocky Ridge Trail. At 35°14.973'N 111°38.028'W the Arizona Trail intersects the Rocky Ridge Trail from the right. Keep going straight here.
    The trail ends where it intersects the Elden Lookout Road at a point that is 2.8 miles *4.5 km* from its beginning. 35°15.281'N 111°37.493'W.

Photo: The trail is rocky, all right, as you can see here. The trail moves later-ally through a pine forest.

Rocky Ridge Trail #153

N

Elevation	7600
7200	
Miles: 2.8	Moderate
Elevation change 400 ft.	

WEATHER
Spring: Fair
Summer: Best
Fall: Good
Winter: Bad, snowy
REPORT

Brookbank Tr.

420

0.8

Schultz Creek Tr.

Oldham Trail #1

T
P
2.0

3

.3

557

Oldham Trail, Easy

2

.5

Driving Distance One Way, Miles: 3.9
Hiking Distance One Way, Miles: 2.8

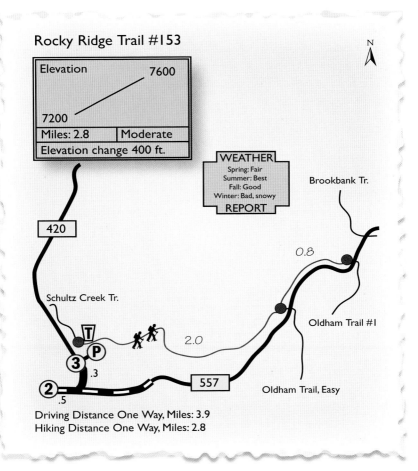

Route 66

Location Map D1
Parks USGS Map
Kaibab Forest Service Map

Driving One-Way/Total: 18.9/37.8 mi. *30.2/60.5 km* (Time 30/60 minutes)
Access Road: All cars, All paved
Hiking One-Way/Total: 0.75/1.5 mi. *1.2/2.4 km* (Time 30/60 minutes)
How Strenuous: Easy   *Total Drive & Hike Time:* 2.0 hours
Features: Walk along a 1931 portion (now closed) of fabled Route 66.

NUTSHELL: A closed strip of Route 66 near Parks has been turned into a hiking trail. You make an easy walk through a pleasant forest to enjoy a bit of history.

DIRECTIONS:
From Flagstaff City Hall (1) Go:

West, then south on Route 66, beneath the railroad overpass. See Access Map, page 10. At 0.5 miles *0.8 km* go right on Route 66. You will soon leave town. At the 5.0 mile *8.0 km* point you will merge onto Interstate-40 West. Drive I-40 West to the 18.0 mile *28.8 km* point to the Parks Exit 178 (2). Turn right and go up to the next stop sign, which intersects old Route 66 (3). Turn right and drive to the 18.9 mile *30.2 km* point, where you will see a signed parking area to your left (4). Turn in and park, 35°15.617'N, 111°55.835'W.

TRAILHEAD: At the parking place.

DESCRIPTION: Route 66 came through this area from its first days, but over the years engineers changed its right-of-way, constantly looking for a better path. The bit of paved road that still goes by the Parks Store is the 1941 route and was used until 1-40 was built in 1964. You will walk the 1931 alignment.

Just east of here was the point where Highway 66 crested at the top of 49 Hill, the absolute high point of Route 66 in its many hundreds of miles, and the old cars really strained to pull this grade. Because of the steepness, engineers changed the alignment in the area to go around a flank of 49 Hill instead of over its top.

You will walk along a disused stretch of old 66 that runs straight downhill. Some of the old pavement survives, but it is crumbling. At the 0.5 mile *0.8 km* point you will see a funky stone building to your left. It was a spring house that provided water to a Forest Service campground. The hike ends near the present paved road, a point where the 1941 route meets the 1931 route. There are two concrete culverts showing how the roads merged here, 35°15.586'N, 111°56.786'W.

Photo: The old alignment of the Mother Road is clearly seen here. While they are not so visible, there are large areas of old gray pavement along the way.

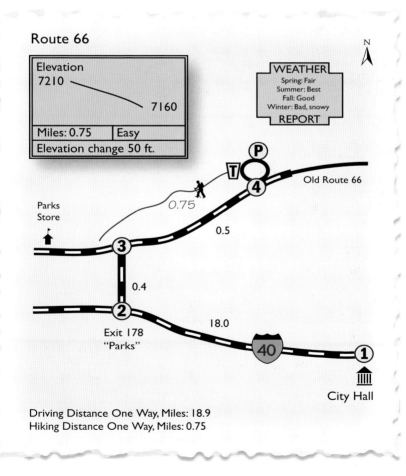

Route 66

Elevation	
7210	
	7160
Miles: 0.75	Easy
Elevation change 50 ft.	

N

WEATHER
Spring: Fair
Summer: Best
Fall: Good
Winter: Bad, snowy
REPORT

Old Route 66

Parks Store

0.75

0.5

0.4

Exit 178
"Parks"

18.0

40

City Hall

Driving Distance One Way, Miles: 18.9
Hiking Distance One Way, Miles: 0.75

Saddle Mountain

Location Map C3
Kendrick Peak & White Horse Hills USGS Maps
Coconino Forest Service Map

Driving One-Way/Total: 24.7/49.4 mi. *39.5/79.0 km* (Time 50/100 minutes)
Access Road: All cars, Last 4.5 miles *7.2 km* fair dirt roads
Hiking One-Way/Total: 2.9/5.8 mi. *4.6/9.3 km* (Time 1.5/3.0 hours)
How Strenuous: Moderate   *Total Drive & Hike Time:* 4 hours 40 min.
Features: Views, Volcanic field

NUTSHELL: Located 25.3 miles *40.5 km* north of Flagstaff, this hike takes you up an abandoned fire lookout road that corkscrews around a mountain, giving 360 degree views.

DIRECTIONS:
From Flagstaff City Hall (1) Go:
   North on Humphreys Street for 0.6 miles *1.0 km*. See Access Map, page 10. Turn left at the light onto Highway 180. At the 20.2 miles *32.3 km* point (MP 236.5), turn right on gravel road FR 514 (2) and drive it to the 22.8 mile *36.5 km* point (3). Turn left on FR 550 and take it to the 24.7 mile *39.5 km* point where FR 550A makes a sharp turn left, going uphill (4). Drive up 550A to the first flat place and park there. 35°26.588'N 111°43.271'W.

TRAILHEAD: Hike the road up the mountain, FR 550A.

DESCRIPTION: Saddle Mountain is an extinct volcano located in a large volcanic field. The excellent views from the top will show you its scope. The mountains that you see in the region are all extinct volcanoes.
   A fire swept Saddle Mountain years ago and burned away some of its tree cover. The fire was a tragedy but it had its good side. As a result of it, you are able to get many unobstructed views. The road winds around the mountain as it climbs, so you are able to see in every direction.
   From the 1920s to the 1960s there was a fire lookout tower on the top of Saddle Mountain and the Forest Service built a decent road to the top of the mountain for access to the tower. The tower was replaced with a transmitter. The road is still maintained so that the transmitter can be serviced. You could drive the road but it is very narrow with no guardrails and almost no turnouts.
   At the top 35°26.318'N 111°43.914'W you can see all the way to the Grand Canyon when you look north. To the east you can see Sunset Crater and the Painted Desert. To the south you see the north face of the San Francisco Peaks. To the west you can see Kendrick Peak. This is a superb viewpoint.

Photo: Views of the San Francisco Peaks that one sees when hiking the Saddle Mountain Trail are superb.

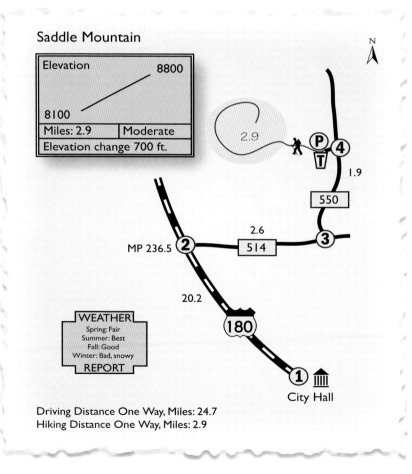

Saddle Mountain

Elevation	8800
8100	
Miles: 2.9	Moderate
Elevation change 700 ft.	

N

2.9

P T 4

1.9

550

2.6
514

MP 236.5 2 3

20.2

WEATHER
Spring: Fair
Summer: Best
Fall: Good
Winter: Bad, snowy
REPORT

180

1 City Hall

Driving Distance One Way, Miles: 24.7
Hiking Distance One Way, Miles: 2.9

Sandys Canyon Trail #137

Location Map E4
Flagstaff East USGS Map
Flagstaff Trails Map©

Driving One-Way/Total: 8.1/16.2 mi. *13.0/25.9 km* (Time 20/40 minutes)
Access Road: All cars, Last 0.2 miles *0.3 km* good gravel road
Hiking One-Way/Total: 1.4/2.8 mi. *2.2/4.5 km* (Time 40/80 minutes)
How Strenuous: Moderate   *Total Drive & Hike Time:* 2 hours
Features: Beautiful canyon, Connection to The Arizona Trail

NUTSHELL: Located south of Flagstaff out on the Lake Mary Road, this hike runs along the rim of Walnut Canyon, then descends to the bottom.

DIRECTIONS:
From Flagstaff City Hall (1) Go:
    West and then south (left) on Route 66 under the railroad overpass. See Access Map, page 10. At 0.5 miles *0.8 km*, go straight on Milton Road. At 1.7 miles *2.7 km* turn right at the light at Forest Meadows. At the next corner turn left on Beulah and follow it out of town. Beulah connects onto Highway 89A. At 2.4 miles *3.8 km* (MP 401.6) turn left on the Lake Mary Road (2). Follow the Lake Mary Road to the 7.9 mile *12.6 km* point, then turn left at the entrance to the Canyon Vista Campground (3), 35°07.366'N 111°35.963'W. Drive through the campground to the trailhead parking lot, at 8.1 miles *13.0 km*, 35°07.540'N 111°35.920'W.

TRAILHEAD: Signed. Located near canyon rim.

DESCRIPTION: You will first walk nothwesterly along the rim of the canyon for 0.6 miles *1.0 km*. This is a very scenic area, with high sandstone cliffs, lava flows and other attractions. At 35°07.883'N, 111°36.367'W the trail turns to the right and will make a fairly steep descent about 200 feet via a pretty side canyon to the floor of Walnut Creek, which carves Walnut Canyon. (Walnut Cyn. National Monument is several miles downstream). You reach the streambed at 0.25 miles *0.4 km*. You cross it, turn left, and hike an old logging railroad grade (it looks like a road) on the other side.
    The trail ends where it intersects the Arizona Trail at 1.4 miles *2.2 km*, 35°08.246'N, 111°35.946'W. This is at a point where the Arizona Trail comes down a cliff face from Marshall Lake (to your right) and then makes a turn, heading northerly to Fisher Point.
    If you have the pep for it, walk the Arizona Trail north for 0.9 miles *1.4 km* to Fisher Point, where there are beautiful striated pinkish cliffs, a half cave and a pond. Walnut Creek makes a bend here and enters an area choked with willows.

Photo: This is a favorite Flagstaff landmark called Fisher Point, a semi-cave, which you can reach via the Sandys Canyon and Arizona Trails.

Sandys Canyon Trail #137

Elevation	
6800 ———____	
_____ 6600	
Miles: 1.4	Moderate
Elevation change 200 ft.	

N ↑

WEATHER
Spring: Fair
Summer: Best
Fall: Good
Winter: Bad, snowy
REPORT

Fisher Point ●

.9

Arizona
Trail

●

City Hall

🏛 ①

1.3

2.4

Arizona
Trail

MP 401.6 ②

Vista Loop Trail

.1

89A

Lake
Mary
Road

P T
△

5.5 ③ .2 Canyon Vista CG

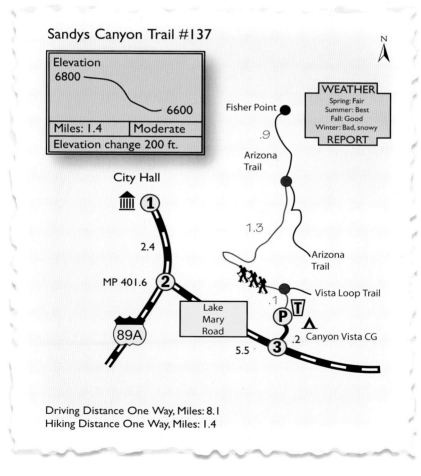

Driving Distance One Way, Miles: 8.1
Hiking Distance One Way, Miles: 1.4

Sandy Seep Trail #129

Location Map D4
Flagstaff East & Sunset Crater West USGS Maps
Flagstaff Trails Map©

Driving One-Way/Total: 7.0/14.0 mi. *11.2/22.4 km* (Time 20/40 minutes)
Access Road: All cars, Last 0.1 miles *0.2 km* good dirt road
Hiking One-Way/Total: 1.5/3.0 mi. *2.4/4.8 km* (Time 1.0/2.0 hours)
How Strenuous: Easy   *Total Drive & Hike Time:* 2 hours 40 min.
Features: Interesting geological formations, Views

NUTSHELL: This hike in the Mt. Elden area northeast of Flagstaff, takes you to an unusual geological feature and provides a connection to other trails in the Mt. Elden system.

DIRECTIONS:
From Flagstaff City Hall (1) Go:
   East, then north on Highway 89. See Access Map, pages 10-11. At 6.5 miles *10.4 km* you will pass a stoplight at the Townsend-Winona Road. Continue on Highway 89 to the 6.9 mile *11.0 km* point (MP 421.1), where you will see a dirt road to the left (2). This is the first road beyond the Townsend-Winona Road intersection. Turn left onto this road and follow it to the parking place at 7.0 miles *11.2 km*.

TRAILHEAD: There is a trail sign at the parking lot at the gate. 35°15.012'N 111°33/737'W.

DESCRIPTION: You will walk along in a northwesterly direction, toward Mt. Elden. The old road that used to take vehicles to Sandy Seep has been blocked off and made into a hiking trail. This means that the path is wide and that the grade is gradual.
   Along the trail you will find many Cliff Roses. When these are in bloom, their fragrance fills the air. You will pass through an area that was burned by a small forest fire. You approach a hill to your right, and the trail begins to wind around it. You will meet the end of the **Christmas Tree Trail** at 1.4 miles *2.2 km* (left) 35°15.305'N 111°34.713'W. Turn right and hike to the 1.5 miles point *2.4 km*, where the Sandy Seep Trail ends and the **Heart Trail** begins, 35°15.398'N 111°34.771'W. The **Little Elden Trail** continues beyond this point.
   We like to hike 0.5 miles *0.8 km* on the Little Elden trail, to the actual Sandy Seep, a beautiful open area, with sandy ground. Between the trail and the side of the tallest white hill, which is capped with a sharp peak, there is a bowl. Water seeps into the bottom of the bowl creating a sometime pond.

Photo: Dick is at the seep's edge. The area forms a bowl which catches water that drains down in the sandy soil. Plants find the water, hence the greenery.

Sandy Seep Trail #129

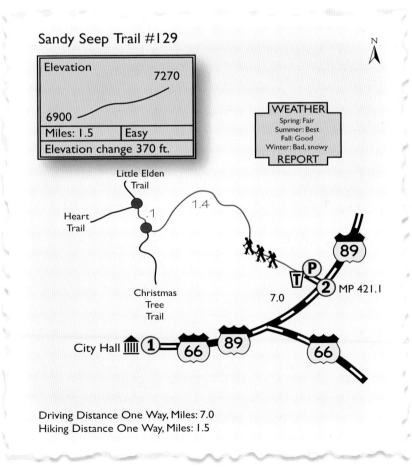

Elevation	
6900	7270
Miles: 1.5	Easy
Elevation change 370 ft.	

WEATHER
Spring: Fair
Summer: Best
Fall: Good
Winter: Bad, snowy
REPORT

N

Little Elden Trail

Heart Trail

.1

1.4

Christmas Tree Trail

City Hall ⛪ ①

66 89

66

89

Ⓣ Ⓟ
② MP 421.1

7.0

Driving Distance One Way, Miles: 7.0
Hiking Distance One Way, Miles: 1.5

Schultz Creek Trail #152

Location Map C3
Humphreys Peak USGS Map
Flagstaff Trails Map©

Driving One-Way/Total: 8.5/17.0 mi. *13.6/27.2 km* (Time 30/60 minutes)
Access Road: All cars, Last 4.5 miles *7.2 km* medium gravel road
Hiking One-Way/Total: 4.2/8.4 mi. *6.7/13.4 km* (Time 2.0/4.0 hours)
How Strenuous: Moderate   *Total Drive & Hike Time:* 5 hours
Features: Scenic creek side trail passes through alpine forest parallel to the Schultz Creek Road

NUTSHELL: This trail starts high on the Schultz Pass Road north of Flagstaff and follows Schultz Creek downhill.

DIRECTIONS:
From Flagstaff City Hall (1) Go:
   North on Humphreys Street for 0.6 miles *1.0 km*. See Access Map, page 10. Turn left at the light onto Highway 180, the Grand Canyon Road. At 3.1 miles *5.0 km* (MP 218.6), turn right on the Schultz Pass Road, FR 420 (2). Stay on it to the 8.5 mile *13.6 km* point, where you turn right at the sign for the Sunset Trail. Park in the lot, 35°17.077'N 111°37.903'W.

TRAILHEAD: You will see a wooden sign for the Sunset Trail. The Schultz Creek Trail runs in the opposite direction. It is on the other side of the entry road marked with a lath, 35°16.938'N 111°37.936'W.

DESCRIPTION: The trail follows the course of the old Schultz Pass Road that ran along at creek level. Down at creek side you will have a delightful ramble. The path is easy to walk, made of soft soil with few rocks. You will see many wildflowers growing in the upper reaches of the trail where the forest is an interesting mixture of pine, aspen, fir and spruce, with willows in the creek.
   The trail is almost always just a stone's throw from the road, which is to your right, and you will see and hear cars pass. This and the presence of bikes mar the natural feeling of this otherwise fine trail.
   At 3.5 miles *5.6 km* you will see several concrete slabs on the site of a 1930s CCC camp. The workers who lived there built the present road. At 3.6 miles *5.8 km* the **Ft. Valley Trail** intersects 35°15.082'N 111°39.927'W. The trail ends at the **Rocky Ridge** Trailhead, 35°14.709'N 111°39.678'W.
   The easy way to do this hike is as a two-car shuttle, parking one car at the Sunset trailhead and the other at the Rocky Ridge trailhead.

Photo: In the late spring hikers are able to enjoy early flowers and running water on this mountain trail.

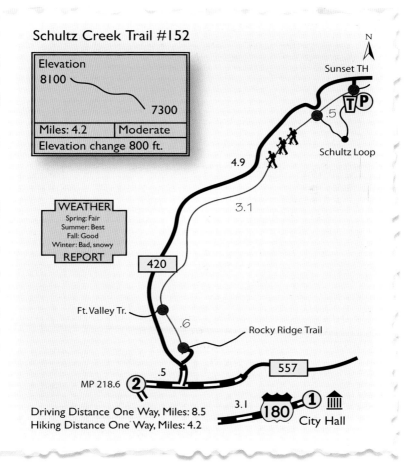

Schultz Creek Trail #152

N

Elevation
8100
7300
| Miles: 4.2 | Moderate |
Elevation change 800 ft.

Sunset TH

T P

.5

Schultz Loop

4.9

3.1

WEATHER
Spring: Fair
Summer: Best
Fall: Good
Winter: Bad, snowy
REPORT

420

Ft. Valley Tr.

.6

Rocky Ridge Trail

557

.5

MP 218.6 2

3.1 180 1 City Hall

Driving Distance One Way, Miles: 8.5
Hiking Distance One Way, Miles: 4.2

Schultz Loop Trail

Location Map C3
Humphreys Peak USGS Map
Flagstaff Trails Map©

Driving One-Way/Total: 8.5/17.0 mi. *13.6/27.2 km* (Time 30/60 minutes)
Access Road: All cars, Last 4.5 miles *7.2 km* medium gravel road
Hiking One-Way/Total: 1.6/3.2 mi. *2.6/5.1 km* (Time 1.0/2.0 hours)
How Strenuous: Easy to moderate   **Total Drive & Hike Time:** 3 hours
Features: A nice easy ramble in the mountains

NUTSHELL: This trail starts at the **Sunset** Trailhead, and makes a triangular loop. The first two legs take you through a beautiful alpine forest to join the **Schultz Creek Trail**, and you walk it back up to the starting point.

DIRECTIONS:
From Flagstaff City Hall (1) Go:
    North on Humphreys Street for 0.6 miles *1.0 km*. See Access Map, page 10. Turn left at the light onto Highway 180, the Grand Canyon Road. At 3.1 miles *5.0 km* (MP 218.6), turn right on the Schultz Pass Road (2). Stay on it to the 8.5 mile *13.6 km* point, where you turn right at the sign for the Sunset Trail. Park in the lot, 35°17.077'N 111°37.903'W.

TRAILHEAD: You come into the parking lot on a road, veering off of it to get to the parking area. Walk back to this road and follow it into the forest. You will find the trailhead at a blocked gate, 35°17.004'N 111°37.953'W.

DESCRIPTION: You start the hike by walking down an old road through a beautiful forest. At 0.3 miles *0.5 km* you reach a fork. Go right. At 0.7 miles *1.1 km* you come to the end of the first leg, where you turn right, 35°16.756'N 111°38.029'W.
    The second leg takes you northwesterly through a fold in the hills, up a fairly steep slope. There is sometimes water running in the creek bed below you. Again the forest is quite beautiful. At 1.1 miles *1.8 km* you join the Schultz Creek Trail at a point just below the Schultz Pass Road, 35°16.818'N 111°38.311'W. But the hike is not over. You must return to the top of the loop. Turn right.
    The third leg takes you uphill back to the Sunset Trail parking area, which you will reach in 1.6 miles *2.6 km*. All of the major points mentioned are marked with signs. This is a very pleasant hike.

Photo: Alpine greenery awaits the hiker on this trail. This shot was taken in the middle of summer when the grasses were green...very inviting.

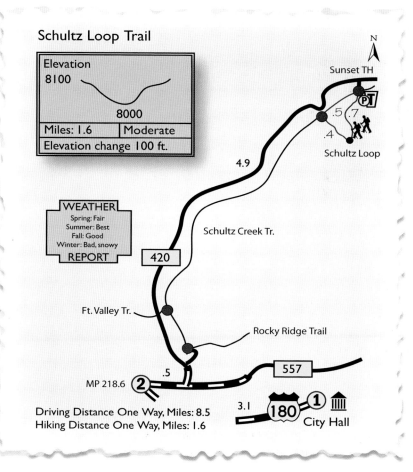

Schultz Loop Trail

Elevation
8100

8000

Miles: 1.6	Moderate
Elevation change 100 ft.	

N

Sunset TH

P

.5 .7

.4

Schultz Loop

4.9

WEATHER
Spring: Fair
Summer: Best
Fall: Good
Winter: Bad, snowy
REPORT

Schultz Creek Tr.

420

Ft. Valley Tr.

Rocky Ridge Trail

557

MP 218.6 2

.5

3.1 180 1 City Hall

Driving Distance One Way, Miles: 8.5
Hiking Distance One Way, Miles: 1.6

Secret Mountain Trail #109

Location Map F2
Loy Butte, Sycamore Point USGS Maps
Coconino Forest Service Map

Driving One Way/Total: 28.9/57.8 mi. *46.2/92.5 km* (Time 1.5/3.0 hours)
Access Road: All cars, Last 25.3 miles *40.5 km* dirt road, rough spots
Hiking One-Way/Total: 1.9/3.8 miles *3.0/6.1 km* (Time 1.0/2.0 hours)
How Strenuous: Moderate   *Total Drive & Hike Time:* 5 hours
Features: Historic cabin, Pristine first growth forest, Views

NUTSHELL: Located on the Mogollon Rim southwest of Flagstaff, this hike takes you to a historic cabin and scenic lookouts. **A personal favorite.**

DIRECTIONS:
From Flagstaff City Hall (1) Go:
    West, then south on Route 66, beneath the railroad overpass. See Access Map, page 10. At 0.5 miles *0.8 km* go right on Route 66. At 2.6 miles *4.2 km* turn left on the Woody Mountain Rd, FR 231 (2). At 16.6 miles *26.6 km* (3), turn right onto FR 538. At 22.3 miles *35.7 km*, the junction with FR 538E, take FR 538 to the left. The road worsens. At 27.7 miles *44.3 km* you will come to the intersection with FR 538K (4). Go left here, on FR 538. At 28.9 miles *46.2 km* the road comes out onto a ridge and goes to the parking area, 34°58.774'N, 111°54.021'W.

TRAILHEAD: Follow the signs at the parking lot.

DESCRIPTION: At 0.4 miles *0.6 km*, you drop onto a saddle where there is a trail junction. The fork to the right is the Loy Canyon Trail (see *Sedona Hikes*). Go straight ahead. You will reach the top of a knob at 0.6 miles *1.0 km,* and then go downhill through an area damaged by fire.
    At 1.0 miles *1.6 km.* on a small bench of land here you will find an old log corral and a dam at Johnson Tank. At 1.8 miles *2.9 km* you will come to another shelf of land, containing Secret Cabin, a corral, and a sometime pond. The cabin is about 20 by 12 feet and only 5 feet high, as several courses of logs have been removed so that no one will try to live in it. This remote place was homesteaded by a family in the 1870s. It was reputedly used thereafter by Mormons hiding from polygamy prosecution. It was a secret place halfway between Sedona and Flagstaff.
    From the cabin go west into the ravine and across it. Walk up 0.1 mile *0.2 km* to a viewpoint on the rim for sensational scenery, 34°57.850'N, 111°54.026'W. We end our hike here. The trail turns left and continues another 1.0 miles *1.6 km,* along the edge of Secret Mountain, 34°57.054'N, 111°53.302'W.

Photo: Spectacular: that's the word for the views from this fine trail. It is in remote and unspoiled country and offers a variety of features.

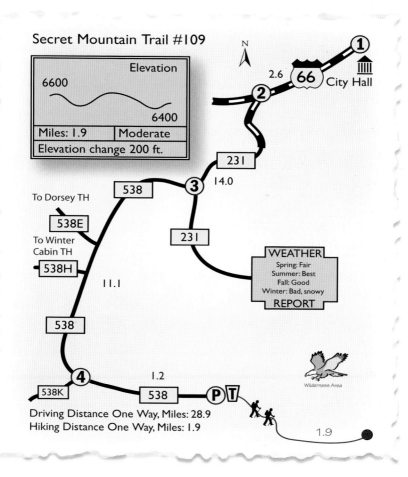

Secret Mountain Trail #109

Elevation

6600

6400

| Miles: 1.9 | Moderate |

Elevation change 200 ft.

N

① 🏛 City Hall

2.6 **66** ②

231

③ 14.0

538

To Dorsey TH

538E

To Winter
Cabin TH

◄ **538H**

231

11.1

WEATHER
Spring: Fair
Summer: Best
Fall: Good
Winter: Bad, snowy
REPORT

538

④

538K

1.2

538 P T

Wilderness Area

Driving Distance One Way, Miles: 28.9
Hiking Distance One Way, Miles: 1.9

1.9

Sinclair Wash Trail

Location Map D3
Flagstaff West USGS Map
Flagstaff Trails Map©

Driving One-Way/Total: 5.1/10.2 mi. *8.2/16.3 km* (Time 15/30 minutes)
Access Road: All cars, All paved
Hiking One-Way: 1.8/3.6 mi. *2.9/5.8 km* (Time 1.0/2.0 hours)
How Strenuous: Easy   ***Total Drive & Hike Time:*** 2.5 hours
Features: Urban trail

NUTSHELL: This is an urban trail in the south part of Flagstaff, running from Ft. Tuthill toward town.

DIRECTIONS:
From Flagstaff City Hall (1) Go:
    West and then south (left) on Route 66 under the railroad overpass. See Access Map, page 10. At 0.5 miles *0.8 km*, go straight on Milton Road. At 1.7 miles *2.7 km* turn right on Forest Meadows and then left on Beulah, which merges into Highway 89A south. Drive Highway 89A to the 4.8 miles *7.7 km* point MP 408.8 (2), where you turn right into Ft. Tuthill on the park's main road and follow the "Trailhead" signs into the big gravel parking lot (3), turn right and then park at the second parking bay, at 5.1 miles *8.2 km*

TRAILHEAD: At the parking area, 35°08.613'N, 111°41.536'W.

DESCRIPTION: Fort Tuthill is a former National Guard facility, now a Coconino County park, known mainly for being the home of the Coconino County Fair. This trail starts at the trailhead for the **Soldiers Trail**, which is contained in the park. The Sinclair Wash Trail runs beyond the park boundary and comes into town.
    You start by walking along a raised roadbed surfaced with red cinders. This is an old logging railroad grade that ran from the mill, located in town, out into the forest. This makes for easy walking. Once you leave the boundaries of Fort Tuthill at 0.6 miles *1.0 km*, you are on the Flagstaff Urban Trail System, though the transition is seamless.
    The walk is not particularly scenic or woodsy, as it runs through areas that have been developed. There are a few "wild" spots, but mostly this is an urban experience. The trail swings away from the old railroad grade as it nears town.
    We end the hike at 1.8 miles *2.9 km*, where it meets West University Heights Drive, 35°10.025'N, 111°40.237'W. Beyond this point the trail is totally urban and we don't enjoy it. It continues to the Wal-Mart parking lot, 35°10.475'N, 111°39.915'W and runs beyond it onto the NAU campus.

Photo: This trail offers a broad clear path from Ft. Tuthill to town. Most of it, as shown here, is located on the bed of an old logging railroad.

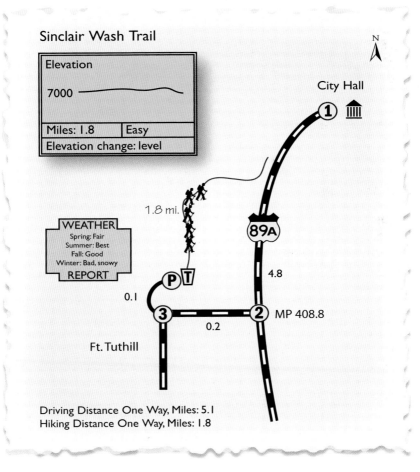

Sinclair Wash Trail

N

Elevation	
7000	
Miles: 1.8	Easy
Elevation change: level	

City Hall

1 🏛

1.8 mi.

89A

WEATHER
Spring: Fair
Summer: Best
Fall: Good
Winter: Bad, snowy
REPORT

P T

4.8

0.1

3

2 MP 408.8

0.2

Ft. Tuthill

Driving Distance One Way, Miles: 5.1
Hiking Distance One Way, Miles: 1.8

Skunk Canyon

Location Map E4
Flagstaff East & Flagstaff West USGS Maps
Flagstaff Trails Map©

Driving One-Way/Total: 4.3/8.6 mi. *6.9/13.8 km* (Time 15/30 minutes)
Access Road: All cars, Last 0.3 mi. *0.5 km* good gravel road
Hiking One-Way/Total: 2.6/5.2 mi. *4.2/8.3 km* (Time 1.0/2.0 hours)
How Strenuous: Moderate   *Total Drive & Hike Time:* 2.5 hours
Features: Near town, Nice canyon

NUTSHELL: In the first part of this hike the canyon is like a grassy valley, but it narrows, the walls steepen, and it becomes more scenic near the end.

DIRECTIONS:
From Flagstaff City Hall (1) Go:
    West and then south (left) on Route 66 under the railroad overpass. See Access Map, page 10. At 0.5 miles *0.8 km*, go straight on Milton Road. At 1.7 miles *2.7 km* turn right at the light at Forest Meadows. At the next corner turn left on Beulah and follow it out of town. Beulah connects onto Highway 89A. At 2.4 miles *3.8 km* (MP 401.6) turn left on the Lake Mary Road (2). Follow the Lake Mary Road to the 4.0 mile *6.4 km* point, then turn left onto SJ Diamond Road (3). Drive in to the 4.3 miles *6.9 km* point and park at the gate, 35°08.611′N 111°38.634′W.

TRAILHEAD: Unmarked. Go through the gate and walk the road up the valley.

DESCRIPTION: Ranchers used to run livestock in Skunk Canyon and the road that you will walk is an old ranch road. At the beginning the canyon doesn't look much like a canyon: it is wide and the walls are low. We have seen deer, elk and antelope in this portion of the hike, so keep your eyes open for wildlife.
    The canyon is quite level and runs in a northeasterly direction to join Walnut Canyon near Fisher Point. You will come to three stock ponds or tanks. Only the last one, Limestone Tank, is named on the USGS map. From Limestone Tank the hike becomes more interesting as the walls of the canyon narrow and become much steeper. There is a nice scenic passage starting where a small stand of aspen grows. Here you enter a narrow place where the vegetation changes to a distinctly alpine mixture of firs and riparian plants, lasting about 0.1 mile *0.2 km*.
    The trail ends at 35°09.319′N 111°36.387′W but an obvious trail continues to the SE. If you walk it, you will meet the end of the **Fay Canyon Trail** in 0.3 miles *0.5 km*. Continue another 0.4 miles *0.6 km* and you will come to Fisher Point on the Arizona Trail. This is a very attractive area, worth exploring, but be sure you pay attention so that you can backtrack and not get confused by the many trails.

Photo: Parts of this trail pass through some typical Flagstaff countryside, spiced in places by interesting areas such as this passage through boulders.

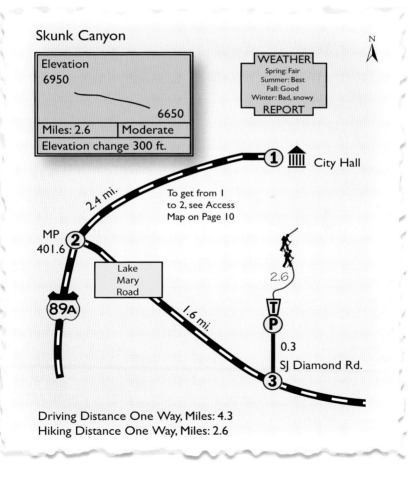

Skunk Canyon

Elevation 6950		
		6650
Miles: 2.6	Moderate	
Elevation change 300 ft.		

WEATHER
Spring: Fair
Summer: Best
Fall: Good
Winter: Bad, snowy
REPORT

N

(1) 🏛 City Hall

2.4 mi.

To get from 1 to 2, see Access Map on Page 10

MP 401.6 (2)

Lake Mary Road

89A

1.6 mi.

2.6

(T)(P)

0.3

SJ Diamond Rd.

(3)

Driving Distance One Way, Miles: 4.3
Hiking Distance One Way, Miles: 2.6

Slate Mountain Trail #128

Location Map B3
Kendrick Peak USGS Map
Coconino Forest Service Map

Driving One-Way/Total: 28.4/56.8 mi. *45.4/90.9 km* (Time 40/80 min)
Access Road: All cars, Last 2.2 miles *3.5 km* good gravel road
Hiking One-Way/Total: 2.5/5.0 mi. *4.0/8.0 km* (Time 80/160 minutes)
How Strenuous: Moderate *Total Drive & Hike Time:* 4 hours
Features: Excellent views, Trailside signs identifying plants

NUTSHELL: Located 29.1 miles *46.6 km* north of Flagstaff, this moderate hike follows an old road to the top of a mountain, with signs identifying local flora posted along the way.

DIRECTIONS:
From Flagstaff City Hall (1) Go:
    North on Humphreys Street for 0.6 miles *1.0 km.* See Access Map, page 10. Turn left at the stoplight onto Highway 180. At 26.2 miles *41.9 km* (MP 242.4), turn left on unpaved road FR 191 (2) and follow it to the 28.1 mile *45.0 km* point (3). Turn right onto the trail access road and drive it to the 28.4 mile *45.4 km* point, where you park, 35°29.144'N, 111°50.177'W.

TRAILHEAD: Hike the road going up the mountain.

DESCRIPTION: Like some other hikes in the book, this road was built to provide access to a fire lookout tower that was later dismantled. The road is now closed for vehicular traffic and makes a fine hiking trail.
    Slate Mountain is an extinct volcano called a rhyolite lava dome. When magma moved up through the Earth's crust to produce this volcano, it tilted up some of the rocks overhead. Along the first several hundred feet of your hike the path and the cut in the adjacent hillside are covered with the dark-rusty-red color of tilted up sandstone and siltstone of some of the same rock formations that are exposed in the walls of the Grand Canyon. Farther up the mountain slope, the rocks are the uniform pale gray of the rhyolite lava dome. Some pieces of the rhyolite exhibit large flat surfaces that mimic those typical of slate (blackboard) which gives the mountain its name.
    A big forest fire in 1996 scorched the bottom of Slate Mountain. As you climb the mountain you wind back and forth to the top, reached at 35°29.671'N, 111°50.525'W. At the top of Slate Mountain there are just a few low-growing pines, so you can see freely in most directions.

Photo: The San Francisco Peaks are the focal point for outdoor activities around Flagstaff, and there are good views of them from Slate Mountain.

Slate Mountain #128

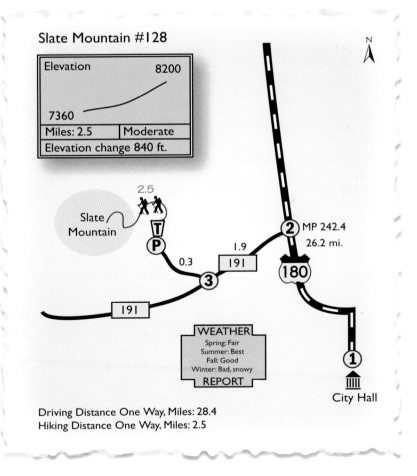

Elevation	8200
7360	
Miles: 2.5	Moderate
Elevation change 840 ft.	

N

2.5

Slate Mountain

T
P

2 MP 242.4
26.2 mi.

1.9
191

0.3

3

180

191

WEATHER
Spring: Fair
Summer: Best
Fall: Good
Winter: Bad, snowy
REPORT

1

City Hall

Driving Distance One Way, Miles: 28.4
Hiking Distance One Way, Miles: 2.5

Soldiers Trail (& Bridge Trail)

Location Map D3
Flagstaff West USGS Map
Flagstaff Trails Map©

Driving One-Way/Total: 5.1/10.2 mi. *8.2/16.3 km* (Time 15/30 minutes)
Access Road: All cars, All paved
Hiking Distance Complete Loop: 6.1 miles *9.8 km* (Time 3.0 hours)
How Strenuous: Moderate   *Total Drive & Hike Time:* 3.5 hours
Features: Easy to reach, Layout permits many variations

NUTSHELL: This trail makes a big winding loop within the boundaries of Ft. Tuthill County Park south of town.

DIRECTIONS:
From Flagstaff City Hall (1) Go:
   West and then south (left) on Route 66 under the railroad overpass. See Access Map, page 10. At 0.5 miles *0.8 km*, go straight on Milton Road. At 1.7 miles *2.7 km* turn right on Forest Meadows and then left on Beulah, which merges into Highway 89A south. Drive Highway 89A to the 4.8 miles *7.7 km* point MP 408.8 (2), where you turn right into Ft. Tuthill on the park's main road and follow the "Trailhead" signs into the big gravel parking lot (3), at 5.0 miles *8.0 km,* turn right and then park at the second parking bay, at 5.1 miles *8.2 km.*

TRAILHEAD: At the sign, 35°08.613'N, 111°41.536'W.

DESCRIPTION: Walk toward town (N) along a raised roadbed surfaced with red gravel **(Sinclair Wash Trail)**. At 0.6 miles *1.0 km* 35°09.041'N, 111°41.430'W, at the park boundary turn left. You will hike west along the park's northern fence, then turn south, where you climb a steep grade.
   At 1.4 miles *2.2 km* you reach a trail junction, 35°08.638'N, 111°41.906'W. The left trail goes to the campground. Turn right and go up the canyon. At 1.6 miles *2.6 km* 35°08.692'N, 111°42.019'W you will reach the north end of the Bridge Trail. (This goes 1.0 miles *1.6 km* south to rejoin the Soldiers Trail).The Soldier Trail goes north, makes an arc and returns to the south. At the 3.7 miles *5.9 km* point you reach the south end of the Bridge Trail, 35°08.233'N, 111°41.775'W.
   The trail soon runs easterly, crosses a cinder road and dips down by the amphitheater. You then turn and hike north parallel to Highway 89A. This area is not very pleasing as you are near the highway, picnic areas and other park facilities. You will close the loop at the 5.5 mile point *8.8 km* where the Soldiers Trail meets the Sinclair Wash Trail. Turn left and walk Sinclar south back to the parking space, for a total of 6.1 miles *9.8 km.*

Photo: Located in a county park close to town, hikers can enjoy an "out-in-the-country" experience on portions of the Soldiers Trail.

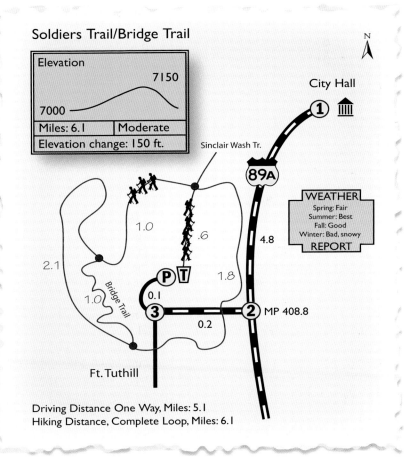

Soldiers Trail/Bridge Trail

N

Elevation	
	7150
7000	
Miles: 6.1	Moderate
Elevation change: 150 ft.	

Sinclair Wash Tr.

City Hall

89A

WEATHER
Spring: Fair
Summer: Best
Fall: Good
Winter: Bad, snowy
REPORT

1.0

.6

4.8

2.1

1.0 Bridge Trail

P T

1.8

0.1

3   **2** MP 408.8

0.2

Ft. Tuthill

Driving Distance One Way, Miles: 5.1
Hiking Distance, Complete Loop, Miles: 6.1

Strawberry Trail

Location Map C5
Strawberry Crater USGS Map
Coconino Forest Service Map

Driving One-Way/Total: 24.8/49.6 mi. *39.7/79.4 km* (Time 40/80 minutes)
Access Road: All cars, Last 5.2 miles *8.3 km* fair gravel road
Hiking Distance, Complete Loop: 2.3 miles *3.7 km* (Time 1.0 hour)
How Strenuous: Hard   ***Total Drive & Hike Time:*** 2 hours 20 min.
Features: Volcano, Painted Desert Views

NUTSHELL: This hike takes you to an extinct volcano north of Flagstaff. You hike to the top of the crater to enjoy great views.

DIRECTIONS:
From Flagstaff City Hall (1) Go:

East, then North on Highway 89. See Access Map, pages 10-11. Follow Highway 89 north out of town. At 19.6 miles *31.4 km* (MP 434.4), nearly at the bottom of a long downgrade, take FR 546 (unpaved) to the right (2). Follow FR 546 easterly to the 22.9 mile *36.6 km* point, where it meets FR 779. Here FR 546 veers to the right (3). Go straight on FR 779, which will take you to Strawberry Crater. You will soon see the crater ahead. At 24.8 miles *39.7 km*, you will reach a huge power line. Just beyond it is the parking area, 35°26.601'N, 111°28.612'W.

TRAILHEAD: At the sign at the parking area.

DESCRIPTION: Formerly known as the Strawberry Crater Trail, the Forest Service changed the trail's name to the Strawberry Trail in 2004.

As you hike, you reach a fork at 0.2 miles *0.3 km*, where there is a sign that says "Strawberry Trail Loop" with an arrow pointing in each direction. We suggest that you go to the left. The trail winds around the west side of the crater, which is one of the more interesting extinct volcanoes that dot the area. You go up the outside wall of the crater and cross through a gap into the interior bowl, where the footing is difficult because of deep black cinders.

The walls of the bowl are decorated with layers of hard rock whose ribs roughly contour around the bowl. These rocks contain clots of lava-fountain spatter that welded to each other when they fell back to Earth, since they were still hot and sticky. Had the clots solidified before falling, they would have accumulated as a pile of loose cinders and volcanic bombs.

You slog up the interior south face and then come down the outside of the crater, curling around the south wall. The views are fine, but the footing difficult. The trail returns to the start of the loop and thence back to the parking place.

Photo: Strawberry Crater dominates the landscape here. Dick is on the flat and level approach and will soon begin to climb the crater.

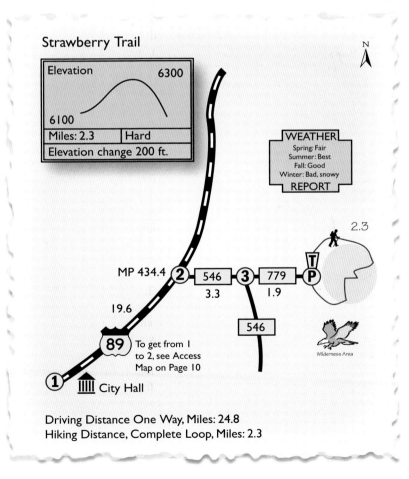

Strawberry Trail

N

Elevation	6300
6100	
Miles: 2.3	Hard
Elevation change 200 ft.	

WEATHER
Spring: Fair
Summer: Best
Fall: Good
Winter: Bad, snowy
REPORT

2.3

MP 434.4 ② 546 ③ 779 P
3.3   1.9

19.6

546

89

To get from 1
to 2, see Access
Map on Page 10

Wilderness Area

① City Hall

Driving Distance One Way, Miles: 24.8
Hiking Distance, Complete Loop, Miles: 2.3

Summit Mountain Trail #68

Location Map D1
Davenport Hill & Williams South USGS Maps
Kaibab (Williams District) Forest Service Map

Driving One-Way/Total: 43.0/86.0 mi. *68.8/137.6 km* (Time 60/120 minutes)
Access Road: All cars, Last 2.6 miles *4.2 km* good gravel roads
Hiking One-Way/Total: 1.1/2.2 mi. *1.8/3.5 km* (Time 45/90 minutes)
How Strenuous: Moderate   *Total Drive & Hike Time:* 3.5 hours
Features: Views

NUTSHELL: This hike takes you to the top of Summit Mountain south of Williams for some great views.

DIRECTIONS:
From Flagstaff City Hall (1) Go:
  West, then south on Route 66 under the railroad. See Access Map, page 10. Follow Route 66 when it turns right at the second stoplight. In 5.0 miles *8.0 km* you will merge onto I-40 West and stay on it to the 29.8 miles *47.7 km* point, the Williams Exit, #165 (2). Take that exit and at the stop sign go left to Williams. Go into town on Railroad Avenue to the 32.2 mile point *51.5 km* where you turn left on Fourth Street (3). As it leaves town its name changes to the Perkinsville Road (County 73). At 40.4 mile *64.6 km* (MP 177), turn left onto FR 110, the White Horse Lake Road (4). Drive FR 110 to the 42.4 mile *67.8 km* point, where you turn right on FR 706 (5). Follow FR 706 to the 43.0 mile *68.8 km* point, where you turn right uphill to the parking area (surrounded by a pole fence), 35°07.816'N, 112°07.577'W.

TRAILHEAD: At the parking place. Marked and signed.

DESCRIPTION: This trail was opened in 1997, following an old trail built in 1916 but thereafter abandoned and forgotten.
  Summit Mountain is not particularly tall as mountains in northern Arizona go, but it is well situated and its top in many places is clear due to steep lava cliffs on which no trees grow.
  The trail winds up the east face through a very nice forest. There are several places where you have good views to the east.
  You will reach the top on the west wide of the mountain, where the forest is still quite thick. The trail ends on a bare crag, 35°07.769'N, 112°08.073'W. From this point you have fine views out over a vast landscape. This trail has been re-routed at the top since the last edition of this book. It no longer comes close to the transmitter towers.

Photo: At the end of the trail, the hiker enjoys a great viewpoint, where a bare cliff face allows views over a vast area.

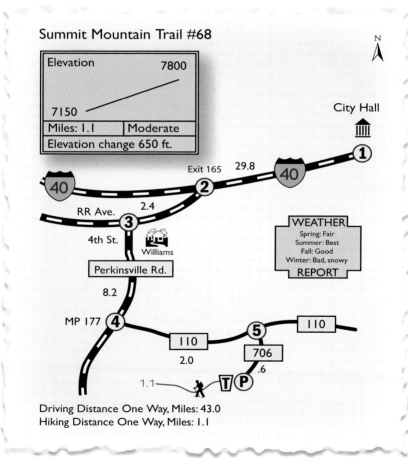

Summit Mountain Trail #68

N

Elevation	7800
7150	
Miles: 1.1	Moderate
Elevation change 650 ft.	

City Hall

🏛

40

Exit 165   29.8   40   ①

②

RR Ave.   2.4
③

4th St.   🏘   Williams

WEATHER
Spring: Fair
Summer: Best
Fall: Good
Winter: Bad, snowy
REPORT

Perkinsville Rd.

8.2

MP 177 ④   ⑤   110

110   706

2.0   .6

1.1   🚶 T P

Driving Distance One Way, Miles: 43.0
Hiking Distance One Way, Miles: 1.1

Sunset Trail #23

Location Map D4
Flagstaff East and Flagstaff West USGS Maps
Flagstaff Trails Map©

Driving One-Way/Total: 8.5/17.0 mi. *13.6/27.2 km* (Time 30/60 minutes)
Access Road: All cars, Last 4.5 miles *7.2 km* medium gravel road
Hiking One-Way/Total: 4.7/9.4 mi. *7.5/15.0 km* (Time 2.5/5.0 hours)
How Strenuous: Hard   *Total Drive & Hike Time:* 6 hours
Features: Views, Variety of scenery, Excellent forests

NUTSHELL: This trail starts on the Schultz Pass Road north of Flagstaff and winds to the Mt. Elden lookout tower. **A personal favorite.**

DIRECTIONS:
From Flagstaff City Hall (1) Go:
    North on Humphreys Street for 0.6 miles *1.0 km.* See Access Map, page 10. Turn left at the light onto Highway 180, the Grand Canyon Road. At 3.1 miles *5.0 km* (MP 218.6), turn right on the Schultz Pass Road, FR 420 (2). Stay on it to the 8.5 mile *13.6 km* point, where you turn right at the sign for the Sunset Trail (3). Park in the lot. 35°17.077'N 111°37.903'W.

TRAILHEAD: Signed at the parking area.

DESCRIPTION: The trail is marked. You walk east toward Schultz Tank, and then reach a signed point, 35°16.990'N 111°37.581'W, where the **Little Elden Trail** ends at a junction with the Sunset Trail. Beyond here you swing south.
    At 1.2 miles *1.9 km* you cross a road and break into a clearing from where you have good views of the San Francisco Peaks (behind you), but soon you are unable to see the Peaks. You follow a shoulder of the Dry Lake Hills to the 2.0 mile *3.2 km* point 35°16.109'N 111°36.662'W, where there is a junction with the **Brookbank Trail.** Take the downhill fork to the left.
    The trail goes down a fold between the Dry Lake Hills and Mt. Elden. At 2.3 miles *3.7 km* you reach the end of the **Little Bear Trail** (left). Then you climb to the top of a ridge on Mt. Elden, passing through an attractive alpine forest. At the ridge line you drop over the other side slightly and walk along below the ridge. At 3.1 miles *5.0 km* you pass the start of the **Heart Trail.** At 3.6 miles *5.8 km*—just above the Elden Lookout Road—you meet the end of the **Upper Oldham Trail.** The trail goes on to the junction with the **Elden Lookout Trail** at 4.7 miles *7.5 km* 35°14.582'N 111°35.716'W, below the Mt. Elden lookout tower. You can climb another 0.3 miles *0.5 km* to the tower, but don't count on being allowed up into the cabin. The tower is at 35°14.460'N 111°35.851'W.

Photo: This fine trail offers a great variety of scenery and moves through very attractive forests.

Sunset Trail #23

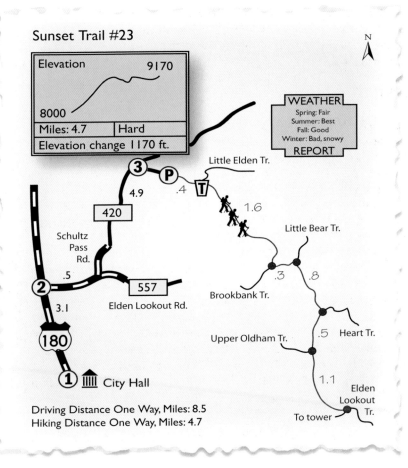

Elevation	9170
Miles: 4.7	Hard
Elevation change 1170 ft.	

8000

WEATHER
Spring: Fair
Summer: Best
Fall: Good
Winter: Bad, snowy
REPORT

Little Elden Tr.

③ P .4 T

4.9 1.6

420

Little Bear Tr.

Schultz
Pass
Rd.

.3 .8

② .5

557 Brookbank Tr.

3.1 Elden Lookout Rd.

.5 Heart Tr.

180 Upper Oldham Tr.

1.1 Elden
Lookout
Tr.

① 🏛 City Hall

To tower

Driving Distance One Way, Miles: 8.5
Hiking Distance One Way, Miles: 4.7

Sycamore Rim Trail

Location Map E1
Davenport Hill and Garland Prairie USGS Maps
Kaibab (Williams District) Forest Service Map

Driving One-Way/Total: 28.2/56.4 mi. *45.1/90.2 km* (Time 1.0/2.0 hours)
Access Road: All cars, Last 10.2 miles *16.3 km* good gravel roads
Hiking Distance, Complete Loop: 12.0 miles *19.2 km* (Time 6.0 hours)
How Strenuous: Hard   **Total Drive & Hike Time**: 8 hours
Features: Cabin and mill ruins, Lily ponds, Historic sites, Views, Waterfall

NUTSHELL: This hike displays the features of the Sycamore Canyon area: spring-fed canyon pools, a waterfall, a huge canyon, a prairie and a hill climb.

DIRECTIONS:
From Flagstaff City Hall (1) Go:
    West, then south on Route 66, beneath the railroad overpass. See Access Map, page 10. At 0.5 miles *0.8 km* turn right on Route 66. At 5.0 miles *8.0 km* merge onto I-40 West. At 18.0 miles *28.8 km* take Exit 178, "Parks". Turn left at stop sign. When you cross the railroad tracks you will be on FR 141. At 27.6 miles *44.2 km* 141 makes a 90° turn to the right. Turn left (S) on FR 131. At 28.2 miles *45.1 km* (2) turn right into the parking area for Dow Springs, 35°09.308'N, 111°58.993'W.

TRAILHEAD: Signed. Go through the opening in the fence.

DESCRIPTION: The Sycamore Rim Trail is a loop. You can start it at five places (see map). We prefer the Dow Spring entry. The trail crosses a canyon and moves along the rim. Water in the canyon bottom forms a chain of pools.
    Beyond these pools, the canyon deepens as you continue along its rim. You reach Sycamore Vista at 35°07.984'N, 112°00.275'W, where you see into Sycamore Canyon. Beyond the vista turnoff you climb a rocky hillside and go down into Big Spring Canyon.
    The next point is Sycamore Falls, a chasm known to climbers as Paradise Forks, 35°08.357'N, 112°01.575'W. When the falls run (spring snowmelt), they are spectacular. From the falls, you walk north along the canyon until you come to Pomeroy Tanks, a series of scenic ponds, 35°09.083'N, 112°01.826'W.
    Beyond Pomeroy Tanks, you will cross the 1863 Overland Trail, Soon after this, you will cross FR 13 and make the 687 foot climb up KA Hill, with good views from the top, 35°10.033'N, 112°00.528'W. Then it's down KA Hill and back to the starting point. On the way you will pass a historic site.
    By using two entry points and two cars, hikers can divide this long trail into smaller portions, as shown on the map.

Photo: This trail offers the most variety of any in the book. Dick is standing at Sycamore Vista taking in the outstanding views.

Sycamore Rim Trail

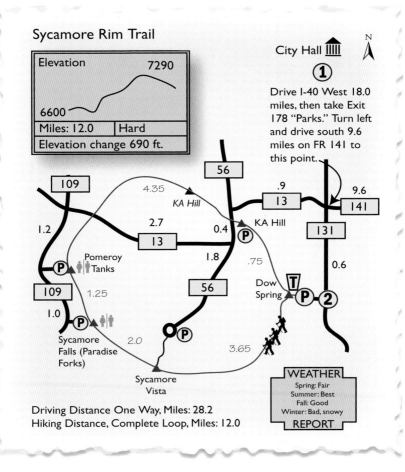

Elevation 7290
6600
Miles: 12.0 | Hard
Elevation change 690 ft.

City Hall 🏛 N

Drive I-40 West 18.0 miles, then take Exit 178 "Parks." Turn left and drive south 9.6 miles on FR 141 to this point.

109
56
4.35
KA Hill
.9
9.6
13
141
1.2
2.7
0.4
KA Hill
13
131
Pomeroy Tanks
1.8
.75
0.6
109
1.25
56
Dow Spring
1.0
Sycamore Falls (Paradise Forks)
2.0
3.65
Sycamore Vista

WEATHER
Spring: Fair
Summer: Best
Fall: Good
Winter: Bad, snowy
REPORT

Driving Distance One Way, Miles: 28.2
Hiking Distance, Complete Loop, Miles: 12.0

Taylor Cabin Trail #35

Location Map F2
Loy Butte, Sycamore Point USGS Maps
Coconino Forest Service Map

Driving One-Way/Total: 29.0/58.0 mi. *46.4/92.8 km* (Time 1.5/3.0 hours)
Access Road: High clearance, 25.4 miles *40.6 km* unpaved, rough spots
Hiking Distance One Way: 2.9/5.8 mi. *4.6/9.3 km* (Time 2.5/5.0 hours)
How Strenuous: Hard   *Total Drive & Hike Time:* 8 hours
Features: Views, Tremendous wild canyons

NUTSHELL: A very steep hike into Sycamore Canyon, so hard, remote and dangerous that it is for experienced, prepared hikers only.

DIRECTIONS:
From Flagstaff City Hall (1) Go:
    West a block on Route 66, then south on Milton. See Access Map, page 10. At 0.5 miles *0.8 km* turn right on Route 66. At 2.6 miles *4.2 km* turn left on the Woody Mountain Road, FR 231 (2). It is paved about 1.0 mile *1.6 km,* then is a cinder road. At 16.6 miles *26.6 km* turn right on FR 538 (3). Drive it to the 26.1 mile *41.8 km* point, where you turn right on FR 538B as it branches off to the right (4) under a huge power line. The road is fair to the 28.25 mile *45.2 km* point but then becomes rough, with exposed rock. It ends at 29.0 miles *46.4 km,* on a ridge, where you park on a wide space to the right, 34°59.048'N, 111°56.629'W. Do not drive farther. If you reach the point where you can see the yellow road barrier, stop and back up to a place where you can turn around.

TRAILHEAD: Walk down the road 0.25 miles *0.4 km,* 34°59.149'N, 111°56.774'W.

DESCRIPTION: The trailhead is on a thin ridge where three trails come together: the Mooney Trail (left: see *Sedona Hikes*), the Taylor Cabin Trail (right) and the **Casner Mountain** trail (straight). The TC Trail is faint at first but soon becomes easy to follow. It zigzags downhill. The trail works its way down through a beautiful forest but is steep and littered with loose rocks, making for hard footing.
    At 1.0 mile *1.6 km,* you reach a flat. From here the trail follows a side canyon, often in the streambed. You must carefully follow cairns and blazes. Hiking here is slow, hard on the feet, almost dangerous. However, you pass through a beautiful red-walled canyon. This side canyon eventually merges into the awesome main canyon of Sycamore, 35°00.207'N, 111°58.193'W. At the bottom you can visit Taylor Cabin, built of native stone and set against the canyon wall. It is a hard additional 1.5 miles *2.4 km* to your left (S), 34°59.299'N, 111°59.300'W.

Photo: The extremely steep and rugged quality of this remote trail are well displayed here, near the top of the trail.

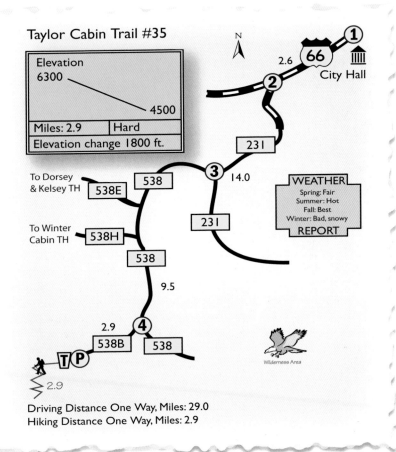

Taylor Cabin Trail #35

Elevation 6300 4500		
Miles: 2.9	Hard	
Elevation change 1800 ft.		

City Hall

2.6 66

231

To Dorsey & Kelsey TH — 538E — 538 — 3 — 14.0

231

To Winter Cabin TH — 538H

538

9.5

WEATHER
Spring: Fair
Summer: Hot
Fall: Best
Winter: Bad, snowy
REPORT

2.9 — 538B — 4 — 538

T P

2.9

Wilderness Area

Driving Distance One Way, Miles: 29.0
Hiking Distance One Way, Miles: 2.9

Veit Springs

Location Map E3
Humphreys Peak USGS Map
Flagstaff Trails Map©

Driving One-Way/Total: 11.6/23.2 mi. *18.6/37.1 km* (Time 30/60 minutes)
Access Road: All cars, All paved
Hiking Distance, Complete Loop: 1.6 miles *2.6 km* (Time 1 hour)
How Strenuous: Easy   ***Total Drive & Hike Time:*** 2 hours
Features: Alpine forests, Historical cabin, Rock art, Springs

NUTSHELL: The hike takes you to an old cabin site on the San Francisco Peaks about 11.8 miles *18.9 km* north of Flagstaff, a lush, peaceful Shangri-La. **A personal favorite.**

DIRECTIONS:
From Flagstaff City Hall (1) Go:
    North on Humphreys Street for 0.6 miles *1.0 km*. See Access Map, page 10. Turn left at the light onto Highway 180, the Grand Canyon Road. Stay on Highway 180 to the 7.1 miles *11.4 km* point (MP 223), and then turn right on the Snow Bowl Road (2). Drive it to the 11.6 miles *18.6 km* point. There you will see a driveway to your right to the parking area. 35°18.586'N 111°43.093'W.

TRAILHEAD: At the gate. There is a nice sign with map.

DESCRIPTION: The trail goes uphill to the right behind the sign, not straight ahead along the blocked jeep road. You will walk on an old road for 0.3 miles *0.5 km* to a trail junction. 35°18.482'N 111°43.055'W. This is where the loop starts. Go left on a footpath. You will walk through an attractive mixed forest until you reach a clearing. When the trail reaches the side of a huge boulder, it becomes confusing. The trail markers indicate that you should go straight ahead. This would put you at the bottom of the loop ready to swing back to the trailhead, and you would miss all the interesting things. Instead take a small path to the left at 35°18.343'N 111°42.806'W. You will immediately come to the cabin remains.
    Go uphill from there and you will come to a flat where there is a spring-fed pond. There are three springs here. The ones you see are Middle Spring in the rock house, and Canadian in the cliff face. If you walk around to your left you will reach Indian Spring, where there is some rock art. 35°18.401'N 1112.788'W.
    Return the way you came and now go down the old road to the Lamar Haines plaque 35°18.329'N 1112.808'W, picking up the trail signs again down there.
    You will then make the return leg of the loop, which is easy walking along an old road.

Photo: We enjoy man-made historic artifacts on our hikes. This spring house over the middle spring is one. This little hike is one of the prettiest in the area.

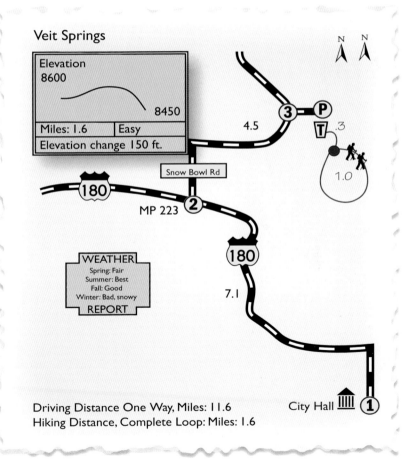

Veit Springs

Elevation
8600

8450

| Miles: 1.6 | Easy |
| Elevation change 150 ft. | |

Snow Bowl Rd

180

MP 223 ②

4.5 ③ Ⓟ
Ⓣ .3

1.0

180

7.1

WEATHER
Spring: Fair
Summer: Best
Fall: Good
Winter: Bad, snowy
REPORT

N N

City Hall ① ①

Driving Distance One Way, Miles: 11.6
Hiking Distance, Complete Loop: Miles: 1.6

Vista Trail

Location Map E4
Flagstaff East & Lower Lake Mary USGS Maps
Flagstaff Trails Map©

Driving One-Way/Total: 8.1/16.2 mi. *13.0/25.9 km* (Time 20/40 minutes)
Access Road: All cars, Last 0.2 miles *0.3 km* good gravel road
Hiking One-Way/Total: 0.6/1.2 mi. *1.0/1.9 km* (Time 20/40 minutes)
How Strenuous: Moderate   *Total Drive & Hike Time:* 1 hour 20 min.
Features: Beautiful canyon, Rock climbing area, Easy to reach

NUTSHELL: Located south of Flagstaff, 8.1 miles *13.0 km* out the Lake Mary Road, this trail zigzags into Walnut Canyon, then crosses to the base of impressive and beautiful limestone and sandstone cliffs, a favorite area for local climbers.

DIRECTIONS:
From Flagstaff City Hall (1) Go:
    West and then south (left) on Route 66 under the railroad overpass. See Access Map, page 10. At 0.5 miles *0.8 km*, go straight on Milton Road. At 1.7 miles *2.7 km* turn right at the light at Forest Meadows. At the next corner turn left on Beulah and follow it out of town. Beulah connects onto Highway 89A. At 2.4 miles *3.8 km* (MP 401.6) turn left on the Lake Mary Road (2). Follow the Lake Mary Road to the 7.9 mile *12.6 km* point, then turn left at the entrance to the Canyon Vista Campground (3). 35°07.366'N 111°35.963'W. Drive through the campground to the trailhead parking lot. 35°07.540'N 111°35.920'W.

TRAILHEAD: At the parking lot.

DESCRIPTION: From the parking area you will see the canyon. Walk out toward the rim on the obvious path. You will come to a trail junction at 0.1 miles *0.2 km* where there is a sign indicating that hikers turn left to use the **Sandys Canyon Trail/Arizona Trail** and straight ahead for the Vista Loop Trail 35°07.637'N 111°35.890'W. Go straight ahead.
    As you start down the trail you will probably see or hear rock climbers. Also notice the interesting lava flow to your left. The trail to the bottom winds down a series of switchbacks. You reach the bottom of the canyon at the 0.4 mile *0.6 km* point 35°07.724'N 111°35.802'W. It's lovely, full of riparian growth—including a bit of poison ivy.
    You follow the trail to the other side, the base of the cliffs. The trail turns left and goes on strongly for a bit, then dwindles. It disappears at the 0.6 mile *1.0 km* point. From this point you have another perspective of the climbing activity and can enjoy the cliffs up close.

Photo: This trail goes down into the upper part of Walnut Canyon, a geologically diverse area of lava flows over beds of limestone and sandstone.

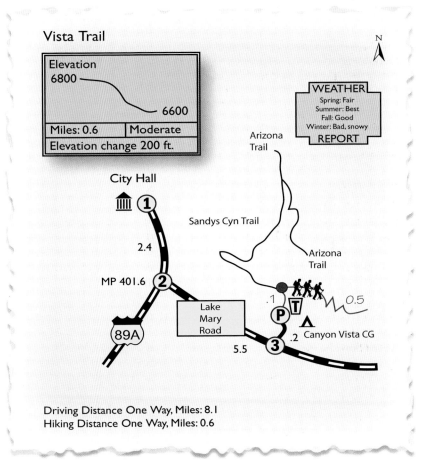

Vista Trail

Elevation	
6800 ⎯⎯⎯⎯⎯⎯⎯⎯⎯ 6600	
Miles: 0.6	Moderate
Elevation change 200 ft.	

N

WEATHER
Spring: Fair
Summer: Best
Fall: Good
Winter: Bad, snowy
REPORT

Arizona Trail

City Hall

(1)

2.4

Sandys Cyn Trail

Arizona Trail

MP 401.6 (2)

Lake Mary Road

.1

P T

0.5

89A

5.5

(3) .2 Canyon Vista CG

Driving Distance One Way, Miles: 8.1
Hiking Distance One Way, Miles: 0.6

Walker Lake

Location Map C3
White Horse Hills & Wing Mt. USGS Maps
Coconino Forest Service Map

Driving One-Way/Total: 21.2/42.4 mi. *33.9/67.8 km* (Time 40/80 minutes)
Access Road: All cars, Last 2.2 miles *3.5 km* good dirt road
Hiking One-Way/Total: 0.5/1.0 mi. *0.8/1.6 km* (Time 30/60 minutes)
How Strenuous: Easy   *Total Drive & Hike Time:* 2 hours 20 min.
Features: Views, Scenic crater, Lake (sometimes)

NUTSHELL: This is a gentle hike up an old ranch road into the crater of an old volcano located northwest of the San Francisco Peaks.

DIRECTIONS:
From Flagstaff City Hall (1) Go:
   North on Humphreys St. 0.6 miles, *1.0 km* to a stoplight. See Access Map, page 10. Turn left onto Highway 180, the road to the Grand Canyon, and follow it out of town to the 19.0 miles *30.4 km* point (2) (MP 235.2). Turn right onto FR 151, the Hart Prairie Road. At the fork at 20.6 miles *33.0 km* (3) turn left on FR 418. At 20.8 miles *33.3 km* turn left on an unmarked dirt road (4) 35°23.079'N 111°44.027'W. Follow this road to the parking area at 21.2 miles *33.9 km* 35°23.285'N 111°43.994'W.

TRAILHEAD: At the parking area you will see the old road going up the mountain, blocked by a barrier. There is a trail marker. You simply hike the road behind the barrier.

DESCRIPTION: The old ranch road to the top and into the crater has been blocked off and turned into a hiking trail. It is wide and easy, holding a gentle grade. You can see that the area was fire damaged. A massive fire raged through here in 1996, so you can get an idea about how long it takes nature to recover from such damage.
   Near the top you may find that fallen fire-killed trees block the road. Look for a path to the right detouring around them. At the top you have two choices: you can walk directly downhill into the bowl or you can go to the right on the old road and descend into the crater on a gentle grade. The GPS reading for the lake is 35°23.538'N 111°44.030'W.
   We like to walk down around the water (if there is any) and if we feel like it, we will bushwhack up to the top of the bare north rim. Because there are no trees there you have extensive views to the north, out over Kendrick Park, Saddle Mountain and dozens of cinder hills.

Photo: The lake, which is not always full, is located in the basin of a volcanic crater, with the San Francisco Peaks visible over the east rim.

Walker Lake

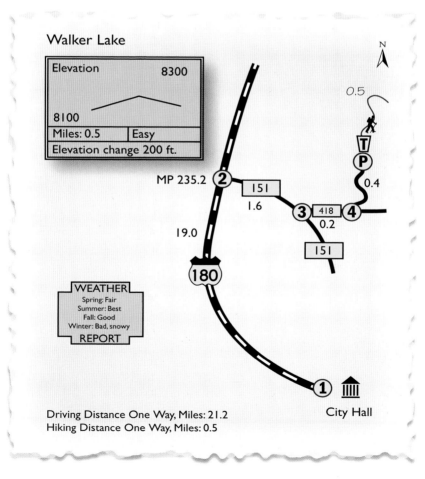

Elevation	8300
8100	
Miles: 0.5	Easy
Elevation change 200 ft.	

MP 235.2

151
1.6

19.0

418
0.2

151

180

WEATHER
Spring: Fair
Summer: Best
Fall: Good
Winter: Bad, snowy
REPORT

0.5

P
0.4

City Hall

Driving Distance One Way, Miles: 21.2
Hiking Distance One Way, Miles: 0.5

Walnut Canyon Trails

Location Map E4
Flagstaff East USGS Map
Coconino Forest Service Map

Driving One-Way/Total: 11.6/23.2 mi. *18.6/37.1 km* (Time 25/50 minutes)
Access Road: All cars, All paved
Hiking Distances: See below
How Strenuous: Easy/Moderate   *Total Drive & Hike Time:* 2.5 hours
Features: Indian ruins, Scenic canyon

NUTSHELL: There are four hiking trails in the Walnut Canyon National Monument, located just a few miles east of Flagstaff. All allow the hiker to enjoy scenery and ruins.

DIRECTIONS:
From Flagstaff City Hall (1) Go:
    East, then north on Hwy 89. See Access Map, pages 10-11. At 4.2 miles *6.7 km* enter I-40, turning left at 4.8 miles *7.7 km*, so that you are on I-40 headed east. At 8.3 miles *13.3 km* (MP 204), take Walnut Canyon, Exit 204 (2). At the stop sign at 8.6 miles *13.8 km* turn right and follow the road to Walnut Canyon. Park at the Visitor Center at 11.6 miles *18.6 km*, 35°10.310'N, 111°30.557'W.

TRAILHEAD: The Visitor Center.

DESCRIPTION:
    Island Trail. Length, 0.8 miles *1.3 km* complete loop, moderate hike. Paved. Elevation change 300 feet. This is the main trail, and is really enjoyable. To take it, you must go into the Visitor Center and pay a fee. Then you go out the back door, where a flight of 240 steps takes you down to a ledge that was undercut by erosion, creating a series of shallow caves. The trail winds around the toe of a ridge and loops back up to the Visitor Center. Along the way you are able to inspect the extensive ruins of ancient cliff dwellings.
    Rim Trail. Length, 0.4 miles *0.6 km*, one way. Level. Paved. Interpretive signs along the trail. This trail moves east along the rim of the canyon. It is a very easy short walk. The scenery is beautiful. You will not walk right by ruins as you do on the other trails, but you can see many ruins across the canyon. On the way back, detour to the Pit House.
    Ranger Cabin and **Ledge Trails**. Reservation required. These are both Ranger-led hikes that you cannot take on your own. They are given in the summer. Check on the website, www.nps.gov/waca for times and availability. These are both quite interesting and well worth the trouble.

Photo: The ancient inhabitants of the area discovered this undercut ledge. All they needed to do to make a dwelling was to fill in the front. Great fun.

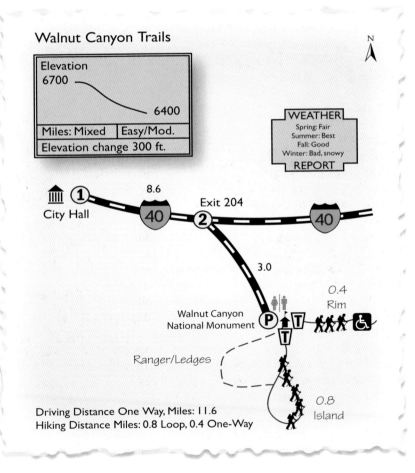

Walnut Canyon Trails

N

Elevation
6700 —
— 6400

Miles: Mixed	Easy/Mod.
Elevation change 300 ft.	

WEATHER
Spring: Fair
Summer: Best
Fall: Good
Winter: Bad, snowy
REPORT

City Hall ① — 8.6 — **40** ② Exit 204 **40**

3.0

0.4
Rim

Walnut Canyon
National Monument P T

Ranger/Ledges

0.8
Island

Driving Distance One Way, Miles: 11.6
Hiking Distance Miles: 0.8 Loop, 0.4 One-Way

Watchable Wildlife Trail

Location Map C2
Kendrick Peak USGS Map
Flagstaff Trails Map©

Driving One-Way/Total: 19.4/38.8 mi. *31.0/62.1 km* (Time 30/60 minutes)
Access Road: All cars, All paved
Hiking Distance, 2 Loops: (1) 0.5 mi./*0.8 km*—20 minutes (2) 1.2 mi./*1.9 km*—
45 minutes. Add time if you stop to read the plaques along the trails.
How Strenuous: Both are easy   **Total Drive & Hike Time:** 1.5 to 2.0 hours
Features: Views of Kendrick Park, Easy to reach, Parking Area, Toilet, Universal
access on shorter paved trail, Explanatory plaques

NUTSHELL: Two connected nature trails, the shorter one paved, making it
accessible to wheelchairs. Both are in a lovely forest.

DIRECTIONS:
From Flagstaff City Hall (1) Go:
   North on Humphreys Street for 0.6 miles *1.0 km*. See Access Map, page 10.
Turn left at the light and drive north on Highway 180, the road to the Grand
Canyon. At 19.4 miles *31.0 km* (2) turn left into the trail parking lot. 35°24.140'
111°45.390'W.

TRAILHEAD: At the parking lot by the toilet.

DESCRIPTION: There are two intersecting loops that can be hiked. The easier
one is paved and is only 0.5 miles *0.8 km* long, and is wheelchair accessible.
Interpretive signs have been placed along both trails. We like nature trails and
always sample them when we have the chance. We think that the signs on this
trail are very well done and are a real help in telling about the cultural and natural
history of the area.
   About midway on the paved loop, the longer unpaved loop goes off to the
right 35°24.092' 111°45.556'W. It runs along the fence line separating the trail
from Kendrick Park, a big open meadow, so there is a nice contrast between the
forest and the park. There are interpretive signs along this trail too.
   At one point, 35°24.093' 111°45.831'W, there is a stile, a set of steps so you
can climb over the fence and make a sidetrip of 0.25 miles *0.4 km* one-way to see
the Ponderosa Pine Management Area. We found this not worthwhile.
   The trail leaves the fence and turns back into the trees, including a nice grove of
aspens, curving back to meet the paved trail. Turn right at this junction 35°23.987'
111°45.536'W and return to the parking lot.

Photo: Dick is standing at a fence along the trail boundary, looking out over
Kendrick Park, a large open meadow that was farmed for many years.

Watchable Wildlife Trail

N

Elevation	
7900 ————————————	
Miles: 0.5/1.2	Both easy
Elevation change: level	

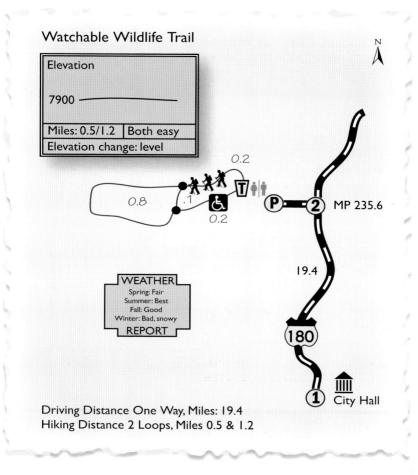

0.2

0.8

.1

0.2

T

P — 2 MP 235.6

19.4

WEATHER
Spring: Fair
Summer: Best
Fall: Good
Winter: Bad, snowy
REPORT

180

1 City Hall

Driving Distance One Way, Miles: 19.4
Hiking Distance 2 Loops, Miles 0.5 & 1.2

Waterline Road #146

Location Map C3
Humphreys Peak & Sunset Crater West USGS Maps
Coconino Forest Service Map

Driving One-Way/Total: 9.4/18.8 mi. *15.0/30.1 km* (Time 30/60 minutes)
Access Road: All cars, Last 5.8 miles *9.3 km* good gravel road
Hiking One-Way/Total: 2.0/4.0 mi. *3.2/6.4 km* (Time 1.0/2.0 hours)
How Strenuous: Moderate   *Total Drive & Hike Time:* 3 hours
Features: High mountains, Interesting tunnel, Excellent views

NUTSHELL: Located 9.4 miles *15.0 km* north of Flagstaff, this moderate hike
takes you through beautiful forests and meadows on the San Francisco Peaks.

DIRECTIONS:
From Flagstaff City Hall (1) Go:
    North on Humphreys St. 0.6 miles *1.0 km.* See Access Map, page 10. Turn left
at the light onto Highway 180, the Grand Canyon Road. At 3.1 miles *5.0 km* (MP
218.6) turn right on the Schultz Pass Road (2). At 3.6 miles *5.8 km* it curves to the
left. The paving ends soon. Drive to the 8.8 mile *14.1 km* point, just beyond the
Weatherford Trail sign. Turn left onto FR 146 (3). It is now 0.7 miles *1.1 km* to
a locked gate where there is no parking or place to turn around. You must park in
a turnout before you go beyond the 0.5 mi. *0.8 km* point.

TRAILHEAD: The gate. Pass through and walk up the road.

DESCRIPTION: The City of Flagstaff and Forest Service maintain FR 146 for
access to the city's watershed, particularly the works at Jack Smith Spring. Only
official motor vehicles may travel the road.
    The grade is gentle, running along the 8,300 foot contour of the mountain, and
makes for easy walking. Although it passes through a thick forest, there are breaks
in the screen of trees, allowing you to look out to the east.
    The road runs for 14.2 miles *22.7 km*, winding around to the north side of the
Peaks. Mountain bikers often go the distance, but it makes a very long hike and
climbs a strenuous 2,300 feet. For a fun day hike, we prefer to stop at the tunnel.
    You will reach the tunnel at 2.0 miles *3.2 km*. At that point the road builders
hit a lava dike and decided to bore through it rather than blast it away. The tunnel
is about 25 feet long, 10 feet wide and 12 feet high, and is quite interesting and
picturesque. The rock formations themselves are interesting and photogenic.
    If you want a longer hike, the next logical destination is Jack Smith Spring at
9.4 miles *15.0 km*, where the **Inner Basin Trail** intersects the Waterline. Otherwise
pick your spot anywhere and turn back at your own comfort point.

---

*Photo: This short tunnel is interesting and makes a natural marker for a place
to end this hike.*

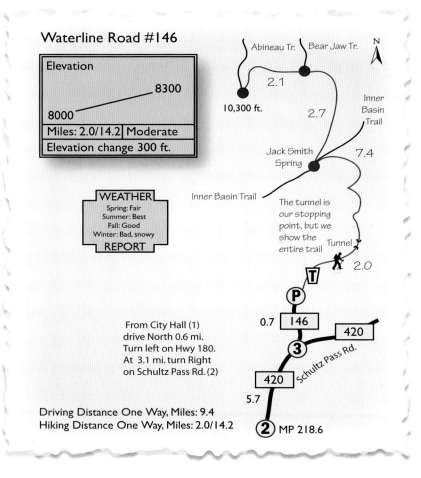

Waterline Road #146

Elevation	
8300	
8000	
Miles: 2.0/14.2	Moderate
Elevation change 300 ft.	

Abineau Tr. Bear Jaw Tr. N

2.1

10,300 ft. 2.7

Inner Basin Trail

Jack Smith Spring 7.4

Inner Basin Trail

WEATHER
Spring: Fair
Summer: Best
Fall: Good
Winter: Bad, snowy
REPORT

The tunnel is our stopping point, but we show the entire trail

Tunnel

2.0

T

P

0.7 **146**

420

From City Hall (1)
drive North 0.6 mi.
Turn left on Hwy 180.
At 3.1 mi. turn Right
on Schultz Pass Rd. (2)

3

Schultz Pass Rd.

420

5.7

Driving Distance One Way, Miles: 9.4
Hiking Distance One Way, Miles: 2.0/14.2

2 MP 218.6

Weatherford Trail #102

Location Map C3
Humphreys Peak USGS Map
Coconino Forest Service Map

Driving One-Way/Total: 13.5/27.0 mi. *21.6/43.2 km* (Time 40/80 minutes)
Access Road: All cars, Last 4.0 miles *6.4 km* rough cinder road
Hiking One-Way/Total: 8.9/17.8 mi. *14.2/28.5 km* (Time 4.5/9.0 hours)
How Strenuous: Hard   *Total Drive & Hike Time:* 10 hrs 20 min.
Features: High mountains, Alpine forests, Excellent views

NUTSHELL: An historic trail to the top of the San Francisco Peaks.

DIRECTIONS:
From Flagstaff City Hall (1) Go:
    North on Humphreys Street 0.6 miles *1.0 km.* See Access Map, page 10. Turn left onto Columbus Avenue which turns into Highway 180. At 7.1 miles *11.4 km* point (MP 223), turn right on the Snow Bowl Road (2). At 9.5 miles *15.2 km* turn right on unpaved FR 522 (the Freidlein Prairie Road) (3). Drive FR 522 to the 13.5 mile *21.6 km* point, and park in the lot, 35°17.822'N, 111°39.086'W.

TRAILHEAD: You will see a blocked road beyond the parking lot. Hike the blocked road.

DESCRIPTION: There are two trailheads for this trail. This one shortens the hike.
    At 0.4 miles *0.6 km* (to your left) you meet the end of the **Kachina Trail**, a favorite hike, 35°17.950'N, 111°38.905'W. Beyond this is a big meadow. Across the meadow you will meet the other approach to the Weatherford trail at 0.7 miles *1.1 km*, 35°18.116'N, 111°38.729'W.
    Next you enter a shaded area framed by aspens. When you see these you will know you are on the historic Weatherford Road.
    The Weatherford Road was built as a private toll road, construction lasting from 1920 to 1928. The Great Depression wiped out any chances of success the road might have had. It fell into disuse and was incorporated into the Kachina Wilderness Area in 1984.
    The trail climbs steadily. You reach Doyle Saddle where you enjoy great views out over the countryside and down into the Inner Basin of the Peaks,
    The trail contours around to meet the **Inner Basin Trail,** at 6.4 miles *10.2 km,* 35°19.625'N, 111°40.041'W. Then it climbs even higher to end where it joins the **Humphreys Trail** at 8.9 miles *14.2 km*, 35°20.104'N, 111°40.900'W. There are superb views from here.

Photo: This is a great trail for seeing fall colors in the aspen groves. The trail moves to the top of the Peaks, breaking out above timberline later on.

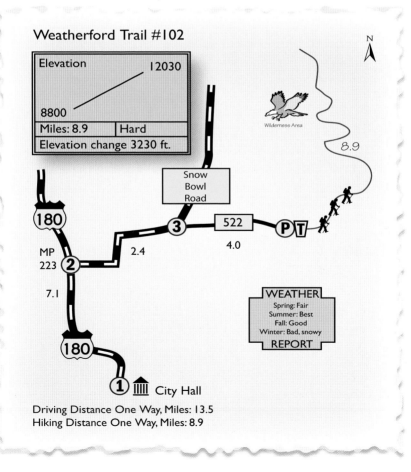

Weatherford Trail #102

Elevation
12030
8800
Miles: 8.9 | Hard
Elevation change 3230 ft.

Wilderness Area

8.9

Snow Bowl Road

180

MP 223

2.4

522

4.0

P T

7.1

WEATHER
Spring: Fair
Summer: Best
Fall: Good
Winter: Bad, snowy
REPORT

180

1 City Hall

Driving Distance One Way, Miles: 13.5
Hiking Distance One Way, Miles: 8.9

Wilson Meadow

Location Map C3
Humphreys Peak and Wing Mountain USGS Maps
Coconino Forest Service Map

Driving One-Way/Total: 14.5/29.0 mi. *23.2/46.4 km* (Time 35/70 minutes)
Access Road: All cars, Last 4.7 miles *7.5 km* good gravel
Hiking One-Way/Total: 1.0/2.0 mi. *1.6/3.2 km* (Time 30/60 minutes)
How Strenuous: Easy   *Total Drive & Hike Time:* 2 hours 10 min.
Features: Aspen groves, Meadow Views

NUTSHELL: Located on the San Francisco Peaks, 14.9 miles *23.8 km* north of
Flagstaff, this easy walk displays the area's alpine beauty.

DIRECTIONS:
From Flagstaff City Hall (1) Go:
   North on Humphreys St. 0.6 miles, *1.0 km* to a stoplight. See Access Map,
page 10. Turn left onto Highway 180, the road to the Grand Canyon, and follow
it out of town. At 9.8 miles *15.7 km* (MP 225.1), turn right onto FR 151, the lower
Hart Prairie Road (2). Drive this gravel road to the 14.3 mile *22.9 km* point (3),
where you turn right onto an unmarked gravel road. Drive to the 14.5 mile *23.2
km* point, the fenced parking lot 35°20.458'N, 111°44.078'W.

TRAILHEAD: At the parking lot. There is no formal system trailhead, but hiking
is welcome. Just walk through the gap between the fence and the gate.

DESCRIPTION: The sign at the parking lot identifies the meadow as a "Wildlife
Habitat Area." There is a reference to the Wilson Foundation on the sign. As we
made this beautiful hike, enjoying the flowers, the meadow and the views, it
occurred to us that it would be fitting to call it Wilson Meadow in honor of The
Wilson Foundation.
   The hike consists of walking a closed road up the meadow. Underground water
flows down this meadow, marked by lines of water-loving shrubs. After 0.5 miles
0.8 km the road disappears near a large metal water tank that captures the water
from a nearby spring, but a single track continues. Just keep hiking toward the top
of the meadow, to the tree line.
   From the 0.5 mile point *0.8 km* you begin to get wonderful views. Turn around
every so often and enjoy them. Three major mountains and an infinity of hills cover
the landscape. The hike ends at a fence at the top of the meadow, 35°20.518'N,
111°43.194'W.
   We have been here at times when the meadow was full of flowers and high
grass.

*Photo: This hike takes you up a mountain meadow to a band of trees. In front
of you are the San Francisco Peaks.*

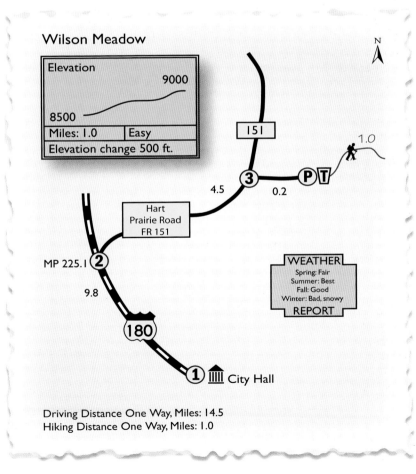

Wilson Meadow

Elevation	
Miles: 1.0	Easy
Elevation change 500 ft.	

9000

8500

151

1.0

3 4.5 0.2 P T

Hart
Prairie Road
FR 151

MP 225.1 2

9.8

WEATHER
Spring: Fair
Summer: Best
Fall: Good
Winter: Bad, snowy
REPORT

180

1 🏛 City Hall

N

Driving Distance One Way, Miles: 14.5
Hiking Distance One Way, Miles: 1.0

Winter Cabin Trail #70

Location Map F2
Sycamore Point USGS Map
Coconino Forest Service Map

Driving One-Way/Total: 26.3/52.6 mi. *42.1/84.2 km* (Time 1.0/2.0 hours)
Access Road: All cars, Last 22.7 miles *36.3 km* dirt road, rough spots
Hiking One-Way/Total: 1.25/2.5 mi. *2.0/4.0 km* (Time 1.0/2.0 hours)
How Strenuous: Moderate   *Total Drive & Hike Time:* 4 hours
Features: Views, Sycamore Canyon access, Historic cowboy cabin

NUTSHELL: An access trail into Sycamore Canyon. There is an interesting cabin in an idyllic glade at the end of the trail.

DIRECTIONS:
From Flagstaff City Hall (1) Go:
    West, then south on Route 66 beneath the railroad overpass. See Access Map, page 10. At 0.5 miles *0.8 km* turn right on Route 66. At 2.6 miles *4.2 km* turn left on Woody Mountain Road, FR 231 (2). It is partly paved. At 16.6 miles *26.6 km* turn right onto FR 538 (3) and follow it to the 22.3 mile *35.7 km* point, a T junction. Turn left on FR 538, and drive to the 25.7 mile *41.1 km* point (4). Turn right on FR 538H, a rough road, and go to its end at 26.3 miles *42.1 km*. Park at the end of the road, 35°01.366'N, 111°55.488'W.

TRAILHEAD: At the parking area. Signed.

DESCRIPTION: The trail passes downward through an attractive mixed forest; with oaks, maples and other trees adding variety to the prevailing Ponderosa pines. The footing is generally good.
    Forest Service signs give the mileage to Winter Cabin as 1.5 miles *2.4 km.* We measured it as 1.25 miles *2.0 km.* The cabin is located in a peaceful glade on a little shelf of land, a remote peaceful paradise far from the cares of the world, at 35°01.962'N, 111°56.109'W.
    The cabin is an old log relic with a corrugated metal roof, still in good condition. The name, Winter Cabin, seems odd because one can't imagine cowboys surviving the heavy snowfalls of winter here, which totally cut off this place from the outside world.
    The cabin is a trail intersection. Trail 70 to the southwest goes 1.5 miles *2.4 km* to Ott Lake, thence another 2.0 miles *3.2 km* into the bottom of Sycamore Canyon. (Don't try hiking into Sycamore Canyon unless you are truly prepared for it. Unprepared people die there). The trail to the west goes to Dorsey Spring , then on to Kelsey Spring on the 7.55 mile *12.1 km* long **Kelsey-Winter Trail.**

Photo: Dick is peering into the interior of the cabin, which is still fairly intact after many years of disuse. The cabin sits in a remote glade.

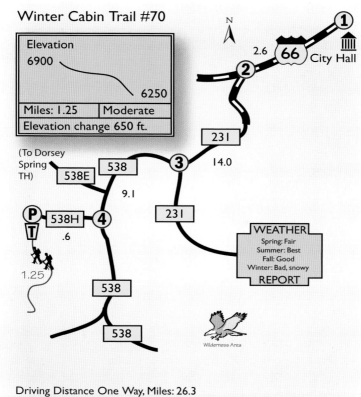

Winter Cabin Trail #70

N

Elevation

6900

6250

Miles: 1.25	Moderate
Elevation change 650 ft.	

2.6 **66** City Hall

2

1

231

(To Dorsey
Spring
TH)

538E **538** **3** 14.0

9.1

P **538H** **4**
T
.6

231

1.25

WEATHER
Spring: Fair
Summer: Best
Fall: Good
Winter: Bad, snowy
REPORT

538

538

Wilderness Area

Driving Distance One Way, Miles: 26.3
Hiking Distance One Way, Miles: 1.25

Wood Trail

Location Map E4
Ashurst Lake, Lower Lake Mary USGS Maps
Flagstaff Trails Map©

Driving One-Way/Total: 15.1/30.2 mi. *24.2/48.3 km* (Time 25/50 minutes)
Access Road: All cars, All paved
Hiking One-Way/Total: 0.5/1.0 mi. *0.8/1.6 km* (Time 20/40 minutes)
How Strenuous: Easy   *Total Drive & Hike Time:* 1.5 hours
Features: Easy to reach, Lake Mary, Fishing, Wheelchair Accessible

NUTSHELL: This paved trail was created for wheelchair access. It winds from a lakeside campground uphill, under the highway, to another campground.

DIRECTIONS:
From Flagstaff City Hall (1) Go:
    West, then south on Route 66 under the railroad overpass. See Access Map, page 10. At 0.5 miles *0.8 km*, a light at a Y intersection, leave Route 66 and go straight on Milton Road. At 1.7 miles *2.7 km* turn right at the light onto Forest Meadows. At the next corner turn left on Beulah and follow it out of town. Beulah connects onto Highway 89A. At the 2.4 miles *3.8 km* point (MP 401.6) turn left at the light onto the Lake Mary Road (2) and follow it to the 15.0 miles *24.0 km* point (MP 331.6) where you turn right on the paved road going down to the Lake Mary Narrows parking lot (3). Drive down to the farthest end of the parking lot at the 15.1 mile *24.2 km* point and park 35°03.857'N 111°30.154'W.

TRAILHEAD: At the parking place. You will see a trail sign.

DESCRIPTION: This all-paved trail starts parallel to the lake. After hugging the shore for about 0.1 mile *0.2 km,* you reach a fork. The right hand fork goes about twenty yards to a picnic table. The left fork is the main trail. Soon you come to a boulder on the right side of the path. A plaque on the boulder reads: "This trail built with support from the Wood Family in Memory of William C. Wood. Access for all." Mr. Wood, who worked for the Forest Service, wanted the forest accessible to everyone. He died in an auto accident in 1992.
    Soon after you pass the boulder, you reach another fork. The right hand fork goes a short distance to a viewpoint. The main trail turns away from the lake here and begins climbing up toward the Lake Mary Road.
    Soon you reach an underpass for hikers and walk right under the road. On the other side the path winds uphill until it comes to a road at the edge of the Lakeview Campground 353.994'N 111°29.931'W. This trail makes an ideal way for campers to walk to the lake safely.

Photo: This trail skirts the shore of Lake Mary, passes through this highway tunnel and winds up in a campground. The tunnel makes it memorable.

Wood Trail

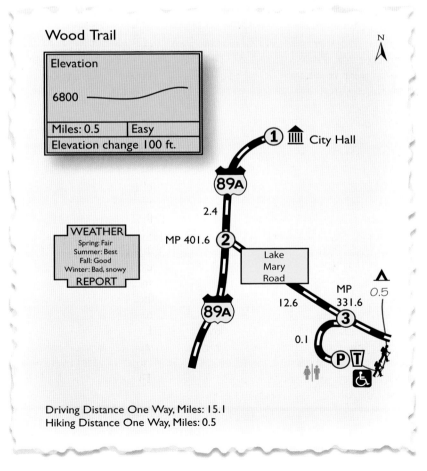

Elevation	
6800	
Miles: 0.5	Easy
Elevation change 100 ft.	

WEATHER
Spring: Fair
Summer: Best
Fall: Good
Winter: Bad, snowy
REPORT

(1) 🏛 City Hall

89A

2.4

MP 401.6 (2)

Lake Mary Road

89A

12.6

MP 331.6

0.5

(3)

0.1

P T

Driving Distance One Way, Miles: 15.1
Hiking Distance One Way, Miles: 0.5

Wupatki Ruin Trail

Location Map C4
Wupatki SW USGS Map
Coconino Forest Service Map

Driving One-Way/Total: 37.8/75.6 mi. *60.5/121.0 km* (Time 1.0/2.0 hours)
Access Road: All cars, All paved
Hiking Distance, Complete Loop: 0.4 miles *0.6 km* (Time 45 minutes)
How Strenuous: Easy   ***Total Drive & Hike Time:*** 2 hours 45 min.
Features: Views, Best pueblo Indian ruins in the Flagstaff area

NUTSHELL: This is a fascinating easy trail starting at the Visitor Center in Wupatki National Monument 37.8 miles *60.5 km* north of Flagstaff. It features pueblo ruins, a ball court, an amphitheater and a unique blow hole.

DIRECTIONS:
From Flagstaff City Hall (1) Go:
East, curving to north on Highway 89. See Access Map, pages 10-11. At 16.4 miles *26.2 km* (MP 430.3) turn right at the entrance to Sunset Crater National Monument (2). At 18.4 miles *29.4 km* stop at the ticket booth to pay admission. Just beyond that is the Visitor Center, worth a look. At 26.0 miles *41.6 km* you reach the Painted Desert Vista. We recommend stopping to enjoy the view. At 37.8 miles *60.5 km* you enter the Wupatki National Monument, which adjoins Sunset Crater. Turn left onto the road to the Wupatki Visitor Center (3). Park in the parking lot. 35°31.218'N 111°22.226'W

TRAILHEAD: The trail starts at the right hand side of the Visitor Center.

DESCRIPTION: This is a favorite excursion for visiting relatives and will keep even the small fry happy.
The ruins are situated on the side of a small valley, where red sandstone provided building materials. The Sinagua Indians fitted their construction around some of the existing boulders so that they could use them to serve as walls and buttresses. Across the valley you can see a couple of small pueblos, but you are not permitted to visit them. Beyond the far end of the valley you can see the Painted Desert.
From the top you walk down to an amphitheater, then to the valley floor to a ball court and a blow hole. The blow hole is wonderful. During the cool hours, the blow hole inhales air. When the day is hot, the blow hole exhales air. The breaths can be quite forceful, causing a loud rushing noise.
While you are at Wupatki we recommend visiting other sites: Wukoki, Lomaki and the Citadel.

Photo: This trail takes you to the primary set of Indians ruins in the Wupatki National Monument, where you will marvel at the handiwork of the ancients.

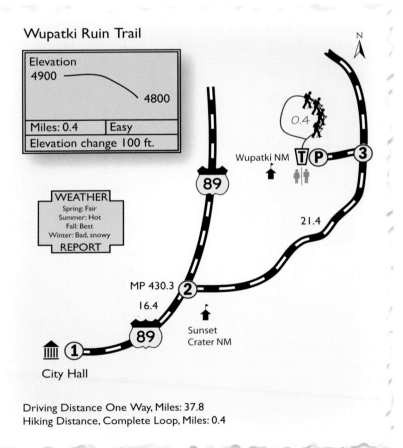

Wupatki Ruin Trail

Elevation	
4900	4800
Miles: 0.4	Easy
Elevation change 100 ft.	

N

0.4

Wupatki NM

T **P** —3

89

21.4

WEATHER
Spring: Fair
Summer: Hot
Fall: Best
Winter: Bad, snowy
REPORT

MP 430.3 —2

16.4

89

Sunset
Crater NM

🏛 —1

City Hall

Driving Distance One Way, Miles: 37.8
Hiking Distance, Complete Loop, Miles: 0.4

Index

Index

Notes